T0381076

50TH ANNIVERSARY
OF
HIS IMPERIAL MAJESTY
HAILE SELASSIE I
FIRST VISIT TO THE UNITED STATES
(1954-2004)

Order this book online at www.trafford.com
or email orders@trafford.com

Most Trafford titles are also available at major online book retailers.

Print information available on the last page.

ISBN: 978-1-4120-3702-0 (SC)

Trafford rev. 08/22/2019

Trafford
PUBLISHING®   www.trafford.com
North America & international
toll-free: 1 888 232 4444 (USA & Canada)
fax: 812 355 4082

İssembly For Rastafari Iniversal Education (IRIE)
At Shashemane Creations, Chicago, IL
111th Earthyear of HIM Haile Selassie
jce2004@hotmail.com.

CONTENTS

The Issembly For Rastafari Iniversal Education (IRIE)

This book is the result of research conducted in Addis Ababa, Ethiopia, from January through September, 2003. The research was made possible by a Repatriation Fellowship provided by the African Caribbean Self-Help Foundation and its subsidiary the Rastafari Goahe Muuzyka Academy, in Addis Ababa. IRIE extends its wholehearted thanks to its Director, Ras Xylon, and to the family and friends of the African Caribbean Self Help Foundation.

All the pictures contained in this book, unless otherwise noted, are from a collection at the Institute of Ethiopian Studies. A special thanks goes to Ato Demeke Berhane, Director of Archives, who collected the material, and Ebrahim Kassa, who digitized all the beautiful photos.

May 25 to July 12, 2004, marks the 50-year Jubilee Anniversary of His Imperial Majesty Emperor Haile Selassie I first visit to the United States in 1954. The 1954 visit marked the 50-year jubilee anniversary of the Treaty of Friendship between Ethiopia and the United States, making this the 100-year centennial anniversary of US-Ethiopian relations.

The Issembly For Rastafari Iniversal Education (IRIE) has taken the responsibility to prepare this book to commemorate this important event. The Ethiopian and American public is especially invited to enjoy the Jubilee Commemoration of this seminal event in American, Ethiopian and world history.

Most Respectfully
Ras Nathaniel, IRIE Coordinator

4

GERMAWI KEDAMAWI HAILE SELASSIE I
KING OF KINGS, LORD OF LORDS,
CONQUERING LION OF JUDAH, LIGHT OF
THIS WORLD, ELECT OF GOD

Emperor of Ethiopia
Defender of the Faith
Grand Cordon of the Order of Solomon
Knight Grand Cross of the Order of Solomon
Knight of the Garter (1954)
Knight Grand Cross of the Order of the Bath
Knight Grand Cross of the Order of St. Michael
and St. George (Hon)
Royal Victorian Chain (1930)
Field Marshal (Hon) of the British Army
Doctor of Laws (Hon) Cambridge (1924)
Doctor of Civil Laws (Hon) Oxford 1954
Grand Cross of the Order
of the Legion of Honor (France)
The Order of the Annunciation
(Order of Italy)
Order of Merit of the Italian Republic
The Order of the Golden Lion (Luxenburg)
The Order of the Seraphines (Sweden)
The Order of the Elephant (Denmark)
Grand Collar of Carlos III (Spain)
The Order of the Savior (Greece)
The Order of Leopold (Belgium)
The Order of Suvorov (USSR)
The Order of St. Olaf (Norway)
The Order of the Star (Yugoslavia)
The Order of the Aztec Eagle (Mexico)
The Order of the Republic 1st Class (Sudan)
The Order of Sansbastian Guillaime (Brazil)
The Order of the Loin
of the Netherlands (Holland)
1st Class Military Order
of the White Lion (Czechoslovakia)
The Order of Military Merit
(Federal Republic of Germany)
Ribbon of the Grand Cross of the Order of
Christ, St. James and Aviz (Portugal)
Honorary Doctor of Laws Awarded by the
following Universities:
Athens (Greece), Banaras (India), Moscow
(USSR), Charles (Czechoslovakia), Columbia,
McGill, Michigan, Howard, Georgetown, (USA),
University of the West Indies (Jamaica)
Montreal, Laval (Canada) (1954)
Honorary Doctor of Agriculture: Bonn
(Germany) (1954)

The year 2004, is the 50th Anniversary of the visit of His Imperial Majesty, Ethiopian Emperor Haile Selassie I, to the United States. His Imperial Majesty's visit was the first ever by an African Emperor and the high point of US-African relations.

The occasion of His Imperial Majesty Haile Selassie I first visit (May 25 to July 12, 1954) was of great national interest to America, and is still of great historical interest today. Three days prior to His Majesty's visit, the U.S. Supreme Court passed the landmark *Brown vs. Board of Education* decision. The United States had just concluded a hydrogen-bomb experiment off the Bikini Islands, heightening world fears about atomic and nuclear annihilation. Even the heavens portended the "times": two astronomical signs of significance occurred during the visit of the King of Kings and Lord of Lords. A Total Solar Eclipse, whereby the New Moon comes between the Sun and the Earth, visible from noon to late afternoon, occurred on June 30, beginning its path in the central part of the United States, passing through Newfoundland, Greenland, southern Scandinavia, western Russia, Persia and terminated in the Indian Ocean. In addition, a rare Mars "Opposition" appeared whereby the Sun, Mars, and Earth formed a straight line with Mars in its closest orbit near the earth (25 million miles). The blood red planet was easily visible between constellations of Sagittarius and Scorpio outshining all stars, including Sirius, the brightest star visible from Earth. With the sun darkened and the war planet shining brightly, the heavens announced the "Cold War" in the new Nuclear Age. In 1954, the United States added the phrase, "One nation under God," to its pledge of allegiance.

All this was happening during the time of "Jim Crow" lynching and segregation in the United States and Colonialism and Apartheid in Africa. The visit of His Imperial Majesty Haile Selassie I was of particular interest, therefore, to African Americans, who saw H.I.M.[1] as the Father and Defender of Africa who had defeated the Fascist aggression against Ethiopia in 1936-1941; and who went on to establish the Organization of African Unity in His capital city of Addis Ababa. Millions of African Americans lined the streets of New York, Washington D.C., Chicago, Seattle, San Francisco, Los Angeles, and New Orleans to see the Emperor. His Imperial Majesty's visit also dominated the American Press.

Thus, it was quite a spectacular event for the United States President, members of His Cabinet and Congress, and full officialdom including Governors, Mayors and University Presidents, to accord every honor to the visiting Emperor of Ethiopia. Most importantly, throughout his tour of America, Haile Selassie I stated repeatedly that the solution to world peace was through the path of "collective security." Bob Marley would eventually make a song ("War") about this doctrine on his album *Exodus*, which *Time* magazine named its "Album of the Millennium".

---

[1] H.I.M. is the abbreviation for "His Imperial Majesty".

THE ETHIOPIAN HERALD

No. 48 - Vol. 11
Saturday, May 22, 1954

A WEEKLY NEWSPAPER
PUBLISHED IN ADDIS ABABA

Subscription Rates (postage included) In Ethiopia:
— 1 year: Eth.$ 6.24 — Six Months: Eth.$ 3.12 —
— Foreign (postage included) 1 year: Eth.$ 9.50 —

PRICE
Eth. 12 Cents

His Imperial Majesty The Emperor Departs For USA As Guest of President Eisenhower

Ethiopian colors saluted by His Imperial Majesty.

His Imperial Majesty converses with H. E. the Prime Minister.

His Imperial Majesty inspects Guard of Honor.

HER IMPERIAL MAJESTY, MEMBERS IMPERIAL FAMILY, DIGNITAIRES, NOTABLES, DIPLOMATIC CORPS AND HUGE CROWDS SEE THE EMPEROR O

His Imperial Majesty Emperor Haile Selassie departed by special plane Tuesday morning at 6.30 on the first stage of His trip to the United States of America as a guest of President Eisenhower.

His Imperial Majesty's arrived at the airport at 6:20 a.m. The Emperor's National Anthem was played by a military band. After alighting from His car, His Imperial Majesty inspected a Guard of Honor of the Imperial Army.

At the airport to bid His Imperial Majesty Godspeed were: Her Imperial Majesty the Empress, His Imperial Highness the Crown Prince, His Imperial Highness the Duke of Harar, other members of the Imperial Family, H.E. Ras Abebe Aragai, Minister of Interior, H.E. Bitwoded Makonnen Endalkatchew, Prime Minister, Cabinet Ministers, high-ranking Churchmen, high-ranking Government and military officials, and an enormous crowd.

(Continued in Column 5)

New Appointments Made by The Emperor Before Departure

HIS IMPERIAL MAJESTY FILLS SEVERAL GOVERNMENT OFFICES

His Imperial Majesty the Emperor was pleased to make the following appointments before His departure for America. The appointments fill many Government posts in different parts of the country and in many branches of the Government service.

B-U-L-L-E-T-I-N

PARIS. — His Majesty Emperor Haile Selassie arrived in Paris Thursday afternoon at Orly airport, accompanied by Prince Sahle Sellassie, the Ministers of Foreign Affairs and Justice and other high-ranking Ethiopians.

His Majesty was welcomed by the Chief of Protocol of the Republic, the Prefect of Seine and by Admiral Barjot. His Majesty the Emperor left for Le Havre to board an American ship for the United States.

TRIPOLI. — His Majesty Emperor Haile Selassie of Ethiopia was received at the airport here last Wednesday by the Prime Minister of Libya, the Governor of Barca and the United States Ambassador. His Majesty the Emperor left for Paris.

KHARTOUM. — His Majesty Emperor Haile Selassie of Ethiopia arrived at Khartoum Wednesday morning at 9:25 on his way to the United States, where he will be the guest of President Eisenhower.

He was received at the airport by the Sudanese Premier Ismail El Azhari and members of his Cabinet, Sir Abdul Bahman El Mahdi, leader of the Umma Independence Party, the Coptic Bishop Abouna Yohannes and many other prominent persons.

His Excellency the Sudanese Premier on behalf of the Sudanese government wished His Imperial Majesty welcome and expressed the respects of the Sudanese people. The Secretary of the Governor-General read a message from the Governor-General, who is at present in Britain. Saied El Marghani, Sudanese religious leader, who is ill, had addressed a message

Full representation of the Diplomatic Corps also were present bid His Imperial Majesty bon voyage.

His Imperial Majesty's entourage included the following persons: His Imperial Highness Prince Sahle Sellassie; H. E. Brigadier General Abyie Abebe, Minister of War; H. E. Tsahafe Tezaz Wolde Giorgis, Minister of Pen and Justice; H.E. Ato Aklilou Habtewold, Minister of Foreign Affairs; H.E. Ato Tafarra Work, His Imperial Majesty's Private Secretary; H. E. Bitwoded Jacques Zervos, Private Physician to His Imperial Majesty; H. E. Colonel Makonnen Denneke, A.D.C.; EndalKatchew Makonnen, Director General in the Ministry of Foreign Affairs and Chief of Protocol; and Mr. John Spencer, Adviser in the Ministry of Foreign Affairs.

His Imperial Majesty Witnesses Demonstration of Well Drilling

OPERATION IS MADE ON SITE OF INTERNATIONAL EXHIBIT

By Our Own Reporter

His Imperial Majesty, accompanied by H. E. Ato Getahun Tessema, Vice-Minister of Commerce and Industry, and Ato De Kifle-Egzy, the Ministry's Liaison Officer to the Point IV Water Resources Program, witnessed a demonstration of well-digging machines in operation on the exhibition grounds opposite the airport last Saturday afternoon.

Two of these machines, each capable

Ethiopian Herald No.48 Vol.11 Saturday May 22, 1954 courtesy of IES

Editorial

HIS IMPERIAL MAJESTY'S AMERICAN VISIT

His Imperial Majesty left last Wednesday morning by special plane enroute to visit the United States of America on the invitation of President Eisenhower. According to the itinerary, His Majesty the Emperor is now on the S. S. United States bound for America to honour the invitation.

There could be no better time than now to make a brief review of Ethiopian-American relations which are longstanding and which have always been cordial. His Imperial Majesty's visit is a climax to a creditable series of mutual contacts which mark the kindred bonds existing between the two friendly nations. As head of State, His Imperial Majesty bears the sincere best wishes of the Ethiopian people for those of the United States.

It was in 1902 that the first Ethiopian-United States commercial convention was signed by Mr. Robert P. Skinner in Addis Ababa. In 1914 the second such treaty was concluded. Since then and today this relationship has continued to deepen and expand.

In the field of politics, His Majesty the Emperor appealed to the United States in July, 1935, to invoke the Kellogg-Briand Pact, four months before the act of aggression against Ethiopia was launched. During the time that many nations recognized Italy's conquest of Ethiopia through that aggression, the United States refused to follow the same policy. Since then together the two countries have stood side by side in the defence of the principle of collective security as well as are they supporters of the United Nations to make it an effective force for the maintenance of world peace.

After the restoration Ethiopia has been able to share concretely in the riches of both heart and hand of the United States. Early, it was through Lend-Lease. Then it was through the United States Technical Mission to Ethiopia in 1944-45 which made a detailed survey of Ethiopia's resources. American nationals were recruited to aid in the reconstruction, such vital fields as banking, education and civil aviation.

More recently general economic and friendship and mutual assistance treaties were signed between the two countries. Point 4 agreements followed through which several important projects have been cooperatively launched. These include the establishment of an Agricultural and Mechanical College, a water resources project, a technical service education programme and well-drilling.

Ethiopia and the United States are friends, and the visit of His Imperial Majesty at the invitation of President Eisenhower is sure to strengthen further this friendship.

Above: This picture was taken at an audience at the Imperial Palace when Dignitaries, Ministers and Notables came to pay their respects to Their Imperial Majesties and wish H.I.M. bon voyage.
Left: *Ethiopian Herald* Editorial about His Imperial Majesty's American Visit. *Ethiopian Herald* No.47 Vol.11 Saturday May 14, 1954 courtesy of IES

H.I.M. HAILE SELASSIE'S VISIT TO THE UNITED STATES

Wednesday, May 19:

6:20 a.m. H.I.M. arrives at airport; military band plays Ethiopian National Anthem H.I.M. inspects a Guard of Honor of the Imperial Army [Note: prior to this H.I.M. made several government and military appointments presumably to "safeguard" Ethiopia during his absence]

Wishing H.I.M. a safe journey were: **Her Imperial Majesty the Empress, H.I.H. the Crown Prince, H.I.H. Duke of Harare**, other members of the Imperial Family, **H.E. Ras Abebe Aragai, Minister of Interior; H.E. Bitwoded Makonnen Endalkatchew, Prime Minister**; Cabinet Ministers; high-ranking churchman; high-ranking government and military officials; and an enormous crowd and full diplomatic corps.

His Imperial Majesty's entourage included: **H.I.H Prince Sahle Selassie; H.H. Princess Sebla Desta; H.E. Brigadier General Abyie Abebe,** Minister of War; **H.E. Tsahafe Tezaz Wolde Guiorguis,** Minister of Pen and Justice; **H.E. Ato Aklilou Habtewold,** Minister of Foreign Affairs; **H.E. Ato Tafarra Work,** H.I.M. Private Secretary; **H.E. Bitwoded Jacques Zervos,** Private Physician to His Imperial Majesty; **H.E. Colonel Makonnen Denneke,** A.D.C.; **Lidj Endalkatchew Makonnen,** Director General in the Ministry of Foreign Affairs and Chief of Protocol; and **Mr. John Spencer,** Adviser in the Ministry of Foreign Affairs.

6:30 a.m. His Majesty departs for Khartoum, Sudan on the White Nile.

9:25 a.m. H.I.M. arrives in Khartoum; received at airport by Sudanese Premier Ismail El Azhari and members of his cabinet, Sir Abdul Rahman EL Mahdi, leader of the Umma Independence Party, the Coptic Bishop Abouna Yohannes and other prominent persons. The Secretary of the Governor General read a message from the Governor General. Saied El Marghani, Sudanese religious leader, addresses a message of welcome.

H.I.M. departs for Tripoli, Libya and arrives Wednesday and was received at the airport by the Prime Minister of Libya, the Governor of Barca, and the United States Ambassador. H.I.M. departs for Paris.

Thursday, May 20: (afternoon): H.I.M. arrives in Paris at Orly Airport. He was welcomed by Chief of Protocol of the Republic, the Prefect of Seine and by Admiral Berjot. Departs to Le Havre to board *S.S. United States*.

9

This is the great American ocean liner "United States" on which His Imperial Majesty crossed the Atlantic Ocean from France to New York. *Ethiopian Herald* No.49 Vol.11 Saturday May 29, 1954 courtesy of IES

In anticipation of H.I.M.'s visit, U.S. Congressman Rep. Abraham J. Muller of New York introduced into the Congressional Record an article by Curtis Luoinski entitled, "In 1936 Haile Selassie First of Ethiopia A Lonely Hero In an International Tragedy This Month He Makes His First Visit to United States, Still Dedicated To His Lonely Task, Ushering His African Domain Into Twentieth Century." The Article appeared in the nationally circulated weekly, "This Week".

Rep. Muller declared, "The world remembers that if the free countries of the world HAD COME TO THE AID OF ETHIOPIA when her sovereignty was endangered by the invasion of [Mussolini and the Fascists] the League of Nations might have survived and WORLD WAR TWO MIGHT HAVE BEEN PREVENTED. THAT SHOULD BE A GOOD OBJECT LESSON TODAY. The United Nations will not survive unless the free countries that make up the United Nations will stand as one against all totalitarians in their attempts to subjugate the world." (Capital emphasis mine) [*Ethiopian Herald* No. 48 vol. II Saturday, May 22, 1954]

US SUPREME COURT DECISION TO DESEGREGATE SCHOOLS

Seven days prior to His Imperial Majesty Haile Selassie's arrival in the United States, the U.S. Supreme Court decided to end segregation in education. The U.S. Supreme Court decision of May 17, 1954 is seen by the Rastafari Family as directly related to H.I.M.'s visit. H.I.M. Haile Selassie was not only King of Kings and Lord of Lords, he was also Minister of Education and the fact that this Royal Black King to whom the US had to pay homage was coming to the United States, where schools were segregated under "Jim Crow" racial discrimination would have proven a colossal embarrassment to the U.S. Therefore, in order to show the King of Kings that the U.S. was making progress in granting equal rights to all without regard to race, the U.S. Supreme Court ruled in favor of desegregation in the *Brown vs. Board of Education* case just seven days prior to His Majesty's arrival in the U.S.

THE ETHIOPIAN HERALD

No. 48-Vol. 11
Saturday, May 22, 1954

A WEEKLY NEWSPAPER
— PUBLISHED IN ADDIS ABABA

Subscription Rates (postage included): In Ethiopia
— 1 years Eth.$ 6.24 — Six Months: Eth.$ 3.12
— Foreign (postage included) 1 years Eth.$ 9.50 —

PRICE
Eth. 12 Cents

His Imperial Majesty The Emperor Departs For USA As Guest of President Eisenhower

Editorial

U. S. SUPREME COURT AGAINST SEGREGATION

So intermeshed are the interests of our present day world that whatever happens in one part may have repercussions in wide areas elsewhere. The United States Supreme Court's decision last Monday on segregated state schools in that country takes its place in this category of events.

The nation's highest judicial body, after two years of debate, has unanimously branded as unconstitutional the segregation of Negro and white children in government-operate schools. Commentators call the decision the most far-reaching and potentially explosive made by the Court since the American Civil War. The forecast range from possible calm acceptance to refusal to accept the constitutional edict.

The decision marks an important stage in the 30 years battle before the courts by the National Association for the Advancement of Coloured People (NAACP). The Association carried 34 cases through the long and expensive road from local courts to the United States Supreme Court. This is the 35th ...

Ethiopian Herald No.48 Vol.11 Saturday May 22, 1954 courtesy of IES

<u>**Tuesday, May 25:**</u>

His Imperial Majesty arrives in New York and makes the following remark:

"It is with the greatest pleasure that I come at last to this great nation held in such universal admiration and affection by my countrymen. It is the first time that a Head of State of Ethiopia and, indeed, the sovereign of an independent state from the great continent of Africa comes to the United States of America. It is significant that, over the years, so many heads of state should have come to visit this great country. Some have come when their homelands have been overrun by an aggressor. Others have come to seek support and aid. All have come as friends and admirers. We have come solely to express to the American people our sincere and profound gratitude and our admiration."

Vice President Richard Nixon greets H.I.M. Haile Selassie I, accompanied by Arthur Radford, Head of Joint Chiefs of Staff.

Ethiopian Herald No.49 Vol.11 Saturday May 29, 1954 courtesy of IES

Wednesday, May 26:

His Imperial Majesty flies to Washington D.C. on President Eisenhower's plane the "Columbine"; arrives at Capital; President Eisenhower salutes H.I.M. as "a defender of freedom"; veteran weathermen described weather as the best they had experienced in years of reporting the arrival of outstanding persons. Stepping from plane, H.I.M. is greeted by Vice President Richard Nixon. Military bands play Ethiopian and American national anthems. America's top military leader, Arthur Radford, Head of Joint Chiefs of Staff accompanies H.I.M. as he inspects U.S. crack military units lined up along the airport runway. "Troops standing with fixed bayonets lined the road from the airport, many of them veterans of the Korean War, in which they fought alongside the Emperor's Imperial Guard." [*Ethiopian Herald* No. 49 Vol. II Saturday, May 29, 1954]

On the way to the White House, the Emperor rode in an open, black limousine with Admiral Arthur Radford and Major General G. Trudeau, American aide to the Emperor. When they reached the north portico of the White House, **President Eisenhower** came down the steps and firmly shook the hand of the Emperor as he alighted from the car. "I am very happy to welcome you here," the President said. Then he escorted the Emperor up the steps where he presented him to Mrs. Eisenhower. **The First Lady** smilingly extended her hand and as she gave the Emperor a firm handshake and said, "We are glad to have you here."

In front of the press, **His Imperial Majesty** said, *"Mr. President, I need scarcely remark that this is a moment to which I have looked forward with the keenest anticipation. For years it has been one of my fondest hopes to be able in person to convey to the President and the people of the United States the expression of profound admiration which I and my people have for your great nation, Mr. President."* **President Eisenhower** replied, "Your Majesty, the American People are honored to have you here on their shores, so that they may salute one who has established a reputation as a defender of freedom and a supporter of progress. For Mrs. Eisenhower and me it is a rare privilege to have you as a guest in this house."

Washington D .C. May 26 1954. After first greetings from President Eisenhower at the entrance to the White House, H.I.M. Haile Selassie I said a few words of greetings in English to the American people for the radio and television networks and the newsreel cameras.

Washington D.C. May 26, 1954. H.I.M. Haile Selassie I presented with a key to the city of Washington by the District of Columbia Commissioner Samuel Spencer in a public ceremony held at the district building shortly after the Emperor and His official party arrived in Washington. The ceremonial Presentation of the Key is a token of hospitable welcome that American cities extend to their most distinguished visitors.

Washington D.C. May 26,1954 After greetings on the veranda of the White House, President Eisenhower ushers HIM Emperor Haile Selassie I, His Highness Prince Sahle Selassie Haile Selassie and Her Highness Princess Seble Desta into the Executive Mansion where they were overnight guests.

American government guest house "Blair House" which was placed at His Imperial Majesty's disposal in Washington D.C.

These photos show H.I.M. Emperor Haile Selassie I going to put a wreath on the Tomb of the "unknown soldier" at Arlington National Cemetery in Washington D.C.

At a luncheon with a joint press and radio committee, **U.S. Assistant Secretary of State Henry Byroade** described Ethiopia as "an example of even-tempered courage and stability" in a disturbed area of the world. Byroade pointed out that Ethiopia, "has been able to move along the paths of modern development without losing her hold on the additional values which make a people great. She has reached the hard decisions which the 20th century forces upon all of us with that inner calm which springs from an acute awareness of national duty and national dignity." Citing Ethiopia's military support of the UN cause in Korea, Byroade said that Ethiopia "was one of the first nations to understand the bitter sacrifices necessitated by collective security." For the Emperor and his people, Byroade asserted, "our hearts reserve that special tribute which free man spontaneously pay to those who ennoble our common human destiny."

At the luncheon, **His Imperial Majesty** says, *"We are convinced and nothing will divert us from this conviction, that collective security can alone be the answer for the future. We voice our idealism not only as a conviction confirmed by experience and sacrifice, but also as a policy that can today be achieved for the good of mankind. . . . That collective security which the League of Nations could not assure to my people has now been gloriously vindicated by the United Nations . . . . . [Ethiopia holds to the principle of collective security] We do so, not only because we feel that it is in the best interest of Ethiopia, materially as well as otherwise to do so, but also because we can see no hope, whatsoever for the future of small nations, unless they are willing to follow our example . . . . Ethiopia feels that her philosophy has been abundantly vindicated. We seek no easy bargain. We commit ourselves resolutely to the challenging struggle of an existence founded in the principle of collective security."*

During a toast at a state dinner at the White House honoring His Imperial Majesty, **President Eisenhower** said, "I think it is safe to say that never has any company here gathered been honored by the presence as their guest of honor of an individual more noted for his fierce defense of freedom and for his courage in defending the independence of his people. . . . .I read once that no individual can really be known to have greatness until he has been tested in adversity. By this test, our guest of honor has established new standards in the world. In five years of adversity, with his country over-run but never conquered, he never lost for one single second his dignity, he never lost his faith in himself, in his people and in his God."

U.S. Secretary of State Mr. Dulles, said, "Ethiopia is the oldest independent country in Africa and it has been a Christian nation since the fourth century. The United States has had diplomatic relations with Ethiopia for over 50 years. The Emperor of Ethiopia has demonstrated since the earliest period of his reign the highest devotion to the principles of collective security. Ethiopia has been a steadfast supporter of the United Nations and the Emperor's countrymen have been among the most courageous comrades-in-arms in Korea. I am confident that the American people will extend the heartiest welcome to the Emperor whom we have long respected and honored."

President Eisenhower In Tribute To Emperor; Calls Him 'Great Man'

WASHINGTON, May 27. — Citing Ethiopian Emperor Haile Selassie for his "fierce defense of freedom", President Eisenhower has paid tribute to the Emperor as a truly great man.

The President expressed his feeling in offering a toast Wednesday night at a state dinner in the White House in honor of the visiting Ethiopian leader.

"I think it is safe to say that never has any company here gathered been honored by the presence as their guest of honor of an individual more noted for his fierce defense of freedom and for his courage in defending the independence of his people," the President asserted.

"I read once," Eisenhower added, "That no individual can really be known to have greatness until he has been tested in adversity. By this test, our guest of honor has established new standards in the world. In five years of adversity, with his country over-run but never conquered, he never lost for one single second his dignity, he never lost his faith in himself, in his people and in his God."

Thanking the President, Emperor Selassie expressed appreciation for American aid in assisting Ethiopia's progressive development. The Emperor asserted, is characteristic of "that extraordinary flexibility of understanding and felicity of spirit which you, as a nation, have been endowed, and of the trust and confidence which you inspire in the minds of others."

Emperor of Ethiopia is Praised By State Department Official

WASHINGTON, May 27. — U. S. Assistant Secretary of State Henry Byroade described Ethiopia today as "an example of even-tempered courage and stability" in a disturbed area of the world.

Introducing Emperor Haile Selassie at a luncheon sponsored by a joint press and radio group, Byroade pointed out that Ethiopia "has been able to move along the paths of modern development without losing her hold on the aditional values which make a people great. She has raced the hard decisions which the 20th century forces upon all of us with that inner calm which springs from an acute awareness of national duty and national dignity."

Citing Ethiopia's military support of the UN cause in Korea, Byroade said that Ethiopia "was one of the first nations to understand the bitter sacrifices necessitated by collective security."

For the Emperor and his people, Byroade asserted, "our hearts reserve that special tribute which free man spontaneously pay to those who ennoble our common human destiny."

For Sale

For Sale — Mercury, 1950 2-door sedan excellent condition, 20,000 miles, never out of Addis. Eth. $ 4,200. Telephone 6366.

Ethiopian Herald No.450 Vol.11 Saturday June 5, 1954 courtesy of IES

Howard University Gives Degree to The Emperor

WASHINGTON, May 28. — Following are remarks by Emperor Haile Selassie today upon receiving an honorary degree at Howard University in Washington:

"It is a great pleasure for me to receive this distinguished award from Howard University.

"I receive it as a tribute to my people and, what is more, as a tribute to the contributions of the peoples of Africa everywhere to the advancement of civilization.

"It is a curious fact, if we reflect upon it for a moment, that Africa has always extend its influence and brought to bear its contribution in the West. From the days of the Ptolemies, the influence of Africa has been to the West. Alexandria a seat of unparalleled learning in ancient times, on the continent of Africa.

"In the same way, Africa has contributed profoundly to the development, both materially and cultural, of the Americas. It is certain that the United States of America would not have reached today its present world stature, were it not, in part, for the enormous labours of Africans whose great descendants are here represented on his occasion. You are continuing that tradition in expanding the new frontiers of thought and science here in these halls of Howard University through the intelligence and efforts of peoples of African origin.

"You have reason to be proud of the role which you are today playing in the life of this great nation and I count it an honour to receive from you this high academic distinction."

Friday, May 28:

Howard University confers upon His Imperial Majesty an Honorary Doctor of Laws degree before 4,000 students, professors, officials of government and education and honored guests. **University President Mordecai Johnson** said, "You have never looked back with vindictiveness; but, in keeping with the great and ancient Christian tradition from which you are descended, and with the simplicity of life and singleness of mind which becomes a Christian monarch, you have worked to restore the life of the people from the devastation made by war and occupation." In reply, **His Imperial Majesty** said, *"It is a great pleasure for me to receive this distinguished award from Howard University. I receive it as a tribute to my people and, what is more, as a tribute to the contributions of the peoples of Africa everywhere to the advancement of civilization. It is a curious fact, if we reflect upon it for a moment, that Africa has always extend its influence and brought to bear its contribution in the West. From the days of the Ptolemies, the influence of Africa has been to the West, Alexandria a seat of unparalleled learning in ancient times, on the continent of Africa. In the same way, Africa has contributed profoundly to the development, both materially and culturally, of the Americas. It is certain that the United States of America would not have reached today its present world stature, were it not, in part, for the enormous labours of Africans whose great descendants are here represented on this occasion. You are continuing that tradition in expanding the new frontiers of thought and science here in these halls of Howard University through the intelligence and efforts of peoples of African origin. You have reason to be proud of the role which you are today playing in the life of this great nation and I count it an honour to receive from you this high academic distinction."*

President Mordecai W. Johnson escorts His Imperial Majesty Haile Selassie, Emperor of Ethiopia, to a special convocation during which the Emperor receives the honorary degree of Doctor of Laws, May 28, 1954. University Archives, Moorland-Spingarn Research Center, Howard University

Emperor Haile Selassie of Ethiopia.
Prints & Photographs Department, Moorland-Spingarn Research Center,
Howard University

Bible - Gift of Haile Selassie, 1954 (illuminated and Amharic).
Museum, Moorland-Spingarn Research Center, Howard University

Joint Sitting of American Congress Addressed by His Imperial Majesty

Following is the text of His Imperial Majesty's speech before a joint sitting of the Congress of the United States:

I count it a privilege to address what is one of the greatest parliaments in the world today — where the forces that make great use of the most powerful of Nations have been and are being brought to bear and where issues of world-wide importance have been decided.

The extent of that power and influence and the rapidity with which you have reached such a summit of importance for the rest of the world are unparalleled in world history and bigger all-conceivable comparison. Two hundred years ago today, as I am speaking, General George Washington won the battle of Fort Necessity, a victory in the gradual forging together of the United States.

His Imperial Majesty Makes Comprehensive Address Before Joint Sitting of Congress of United States

(Continued from page 1)

Of what interest is it to you then, you may well ask, that I, the head of what must be for you a small and remote country, should appear before you in the midst of your deliberations? I do not take it upon myself to point out why Ethiopia is important to the United States — that you can best judge for yourselves, but rather, to explain to you with brevity, the circumstances which make Ethiopia a significant factor in world politics. Since so much of world politics is, today, influenced by the decisions which you, Members of Congress, reach, here in these halls, it is, perhaps, not unimportant that I set out these considerations for you.

A moment ago, I remarked that, for you, Ethiopia must appear to be a small and remote country. Both of these terms are purely relative. In fact, so far as size is concerned, Ethiopia has exactly the area and population of your entire Pacific Far-West consisting of the states of California, Oregon, Washington and also Idaho. We are remote, perhaps, only in the sense that We enjoy a secure position on the high plateau of East Africa protected by the Red Sea and our mountain fastnesses. However, by the numerous air lines that link us with the rest of the world, it is possible to arrive in Washington from Addis Ababa in less than two days.

By one of those strange parallels of history, Ethiopia and a certain well-known country of the Far East who both took active hostile detrimental and strategic positions in their respective areas of the world, both...

American Congress is Addressed By Visiting Emperor of Ethiopia

(Continued from Page 2, Col. 6)

through which the ideas and influences of the continent of Africa should pass to the East and vice versa.

people, and our common comradeship in arms that have laid a very sure and lasting basis for friendship between a great and a small country.

...and to pursue their education.

Finally, through the return in 1952 of its historic ports on the Red Sea and of the long lost territory of Eritrea, Ethiopia has not only regained access to the sea, but has been one of the few states in the post-war world to have regained lost territory pursuant to post-war treaties and in application of peaceful methods.

We have thus become a land of expanding opportunities where the American pioneering spirit, ingenuity and technical abilities have been and will continue to be welcomed.

A thousand year old history of struggles to defend the territorial integrity of our country, the long fight for liberation two decades ago and the recent campaigns in Korea have given our army an esprit de corps and a fighting spirit that, I believe, can stand, without misgiving, for comparison. Today, our fighting forces are among the largest and best trained in the Middle East.

The struggle for liberation served to strengthen Korea have given our army esprit de corps and at that time we have made significant advances in social progress. Unlike many other countries, Ethiopia has long been a nation of small, rather than of large landowners. Moreover, a profoundly democratic tradition has assured in the past, as it assures today, the rise to the highest posts of responsibility in the government, of men, of the humblest of origins.

It is but natural, therefore, that a state which has existed for three thousand years, which has regained its independence by the blood of its patriots, which commands the allegiance and loyalty of even its most humble subjects, and which enjoys an unusually sound economy, should have a regime of marked stability in that area of the world where stability is so frequently absent today.

Such is the state of Ethiopia today about which I am speaking. It is against this background that I want to talk to you of Ethiopia as a factor in world politics. Her geographic location is of great significance, with a long shore line and its archipelago of hundreds of islands, Ethiopia occupies a unique position on the most critical but important of strategic line of communications in the world, that which passes through the Red Sea.

H.I.M. Haile Selassie addresses joint session of America Congress

"I count it a privilege to address what is one of the greatest parliaments in the world today – where the forces that make great one of the most powerful of Nations have been and are being brought to bear and where issues of world-wide importance have been decided.

The extent of that power and influence and the rapidity with which you have reached such a summit of importance for the rest of the world are unparalleled in world history and begger all conceivable comparisons. Two hundred years ago today, as I am speaking, General George Washington won the battle of Fort Necessity, a victory in the gradual forging together of the United States.

What a phenomenal progress has been made in that interval of two hundred years, an interval which – you may pardon me as representative of one of the most ancient nations in the world – is surely but a surprisingly short passage of time.

So great are your power and wealth that the budget of a single American city often equals that of an entire nation.

As in the case of other countries, you gave us lend-lease assistance during the war and, at present, both mutual security and technical assistance. Yet, so vast are your power and resources that even after deducting all expenses of the Federal Government, you have met the costs of this assistance in one-quarter of an hour – fifteen minutes – of your annual production.

Of what interest is it to you, then, you may well ask, that I, the head of what must be for you a small and remote country, should appear before you in the midst of your deliberations? I do not take it upon myself to point out why Ethiopia is important to the United States – that you can best judge for yourselves, but, rather, to explain to you with brevity, the circumstances which make Ethiopia a significant factor in world politics. Since so much of world politics is, today, influenced by the decisions which you, Members of Congress, reach, here in these halls, it is, perhaps, not unimportant that I set out these considerations for you.

A moment ago, I remarked that, for you, Ethiopia must appear to be a small and remote country. Both of these terms are purely relative. In fact, so far as size is concerned, Ethiopia has exactly the area and population of your entire Pacific Far-West consisting of the states of California, Oregon, Washington and also Idaho. We are remote, perhaps, only in the sense that We enjoy a secure position on the high plateau of East Africa protected by the Red Sea and our mountain Fastnesses. However, by the numerous air lines that link us with the rest of the world, it is possible to arrive in Washington from Addis Ababa in less than two days.

By one of those strange parallels of history, Ethiopia and a certain well-known country of the Far East who both enjoy highly defensible and strategic positions in their respective areas of the world, both, for similar reasons, simultaneously, at the beginning of the seventeenth century came out of their period of isolation. As in the case of the other country, that isolation came to an end in the latter half of the nineteenth century, with this difference that, upon abandoning her policy of isolation, she was immediately called upon to defend against tremendous odds, her thousand-year-old independence. Indeed, so bitter has been this struggle against foreign aggrandizement, that were it not for our persistence and for the enormous social, economic and material advance Ethiopia has made in the interval, and particularly since the last war, Ethiopia might very well have turned to her policy of isolation.

In consequence, in many respects, and particularly since the last world war, Ethiopia has become a new frontier of widely expanding opportunities, notwithstanding the tremendous set-back which we suffered in the unprovoked invasion of our country nineteen years ago and the long years of unaided struggle against an infinitely stronger enemy. The last seventeen years have seen the quadrupling of our foreign trade, currency and foreign exchange holdings. Holdings of American dollars have increased ten times over. The Ethiopian dollar has become the only US dollar-based currency in the Middle East today. The assets of our national bank of issue have increased one thousand percent. Blessed with what is perhaps the most fertile soil in Africa, well-watered, and with a wide variety of climates ranging from temperate on the plateau, to the tropical in the valleys, Ethiopia can grow throughout the year crops, normally raised only in widely separated areas of the earth's surface.

Since the war, Ethiopia has become the granary of the Middle East, as well as the only exporter of meat, cereals and vegetables. Whereas at the end of the war, every educational facility had been destroyed, today, schools are springing up throughout the land, the enrollment has quadrupled and, as in the pioneer days in the United States, and indeed, I presume, as in the lives of many of the distinguished members of Congress here present, school-children, in their zeal for education, take all sorts of work in order to earn money to purchase text books and to pursue their education.

Finally, through the return in 1952 of its historic ports on the Red Sea and of the long-lost territory of Eritrea, Ethiopia has not only regained access to the sea, but has been one of the few states in the post-war world to have regained lost territory pursuant to post-war treaties and in application of peaceful means methods.

We have thus become a land of expanding opportunities where the American pioneering spirit, ingenuity and technical abilities have been and will continue to be welcomed

A thousand year old history of struggles to defend the territorial integrity of our country, the long fight for liberation two decades ago, and the recent campaign in Korea have given our army an *esprit de corps* and a fighting spirit that, I believe, can stand, without any misgiving, for comparison. Today, our fighting forces are among the largest and best trained in the Middle East.

The struggle for liberation served to strengthen Korea have given our army *esprit de corps* and during that time we have made significant advances in social progress. Unlike many other countries, Ethiopia has long been a nation of small, rather than of large landowners. Moreover, a profoundly democratic tradition has assured in the past, as it assures today, the rise to the highest posts of responsibility in the government, of men of the humblest origins.

It is but natural, therefore, that a state which has existed for three thousand years, which has regained its independence by the blood of its patriots, which commands the allegiance and loyalty of even its most lowly subjects, and which enjoys an unusually sound economy, should have a regime of marked stability in that area of the world where stability is so frequently absent today.

Such is the state of Ethiopia today about which I am speaking. It is against this background that I wish to talk to you of Ethiopia as a factor in world politics. Her geographic location is of great significance, with her long shore line and its archipelago of hundreds of islands. Ethiopia occupies a unique position on the most constricted but important strategic line of communications in the world, that which passes through the Red Sea. She also lies on the other most strategic line of communication in the world, namely, the world band of telecommunications which, because of natural phenomena, circles the world at the Equator.

However, in yet a perhaps broader sense is Ethiopia's geographical position of significance. Through her location on the shores of the Red Sea and in the horn of East Africa, Ethiopia has profound historical ties with the rest of the Middle East as well as with Africa. In this respect she stands in a completely unique position. Her culture and social structure were founded in the mingling of her original culture and civilization with the Hamitic and Semitic migrations into Africa from the Arabian peninsula, and, in fact, today, our language, Amharic, is a member of that large family of Hamitic and Semitic tongues and, therefore, intimately related to Hebrew and Arabic. Indeed, at one time Ethiopia extended to both sides of the Red Sea as well as north to Upper Egypt. It was, therefore, not without reason that, during the Middle Ages the Emperor (unreadable)

On the other hand, three thousand years of history make Ethiopia a profoundly African state in all that that term implies. In the United Nations, she has been to the forefront in the defense of Africa's racial, economic and social interests. Finally, both culturally and geographically, Ethiopia serves to a unique degree as the link between the Middle East and Africa. Situated in the Horn of Africa, and along the shores of the Red Sea, with the desert area of Africa to the north and west, it is but natural that Ethiopia should be the (unreadable) known as 'he who maintains order between the Christians and the Moslems.' A profound comprehension of and sympathy with other states of the Middle East naturally inspires Ethiopian national policies, through which the ideas and influences of the continent of Africa should pass to the East and vice versa. Thus, our social and political outlook and orientation became important not just in terms of Middle Eastern and African but also, in terms of world politics – and this leads me to point to a factor which I consider to be of due significance. We have a profound orientation towards the west. This consideration alone, although there are others, would suffice to explain this result. The two Americas and the continent of Europe together constitute exactly one-third of the land masses of the world. It is in this one-third that are concentrated the peoples of the Christian Faith. With but rare exceptions Christianity does not extend beyond the confines of the Mediterranean. Here, I find it significant that, in point of fact, in this remaining two-thirds of the earth's surface, Ethiopia is the state having the largest Christian population and is by far the largest Christian state in the Middle East. In Fact, Ethiopia is unique among the nations of the world in that it is, today, the one remaining Christian state that can trace her history unbroken as a Christian polity from the days when the Roman Empire itself was still a vigorous reality.

The strength of the Christian tradition has been of vital significance in our national history, and as a force for the unification of the Empire of Ethiopia. It is this force which gives us, among the other countries of the Middle East, a profound orientation toward the West. We read the same Bible. We speak a common spiritual language.

It is this heritage of ideals and principles that has excluded from our conscious, indeed, from our unconscious processes, the possibility of compromising with those principles which We hold sacred.

We have sought to remain faithful to the principle of respect for the rights of others, and the right of each people to an independent existence. We, like you, are profoundly opposed to the un-Christian use of force and are, as you, attached to a concept of the pacific settlement of disputes.

Our lone struggle before the outbreak of the last world catastrophe, as, indeed, our recent participation in the combined efforts and the glorious comradeship in arms in Korea have marked us, like you, in giving more than lip service to these ideals. It is your deep comprehension of our ideals and struggles in which it has been my privilege to lead, at times not without heartbreak, my beloved people, and our common comradeship in arms that have laid a very sure and lasting basis for friendship between a great and small country.

Last year, we concluded with you a new treaty of friendship, commerce and navigation designed to assure to American business enterprise expanded opportunities in Ethiopia. Our dollar-based currency is also there to assure the ready return to the United States of the profits of their investments. We have entrusted to American enterprise the development of our civil aviation which has surpassed all expectations. To American enterprise we have confided the exploitation of our oil resources as well as of our gold deposits. Although my country is 8,000 miles removed from the eastern seaboard of the United States, United States exports to Ethiopia have, notwithstanding this heavy handicap, pushed forward to the forefront in Ethiopia.

Conversely, the United States stands in first rank of countries to whom we export. Ethiopia has, from the province of Kaffa, given the world the name and product of coffee. The coffee which you drink attains its unique and pleasant American flavor, in part, at least, through the added mixture of Ethiopian coffee. American shoes are made, in part at least, from Ethiopian goatskins which are principally exported to the United States.

On the other hand you have given us valuable support, not only in lend-lease assistance during the war, and today through mutual security and technical assistance agreements, but you have also powerfully aided us in obtaining rectification of long-standing injustices. If, today, the brother territory of Eritrea stands finally united under the Crown and if Ethiopia has regained her shoreline on the Red Sea, it has been due, in no small measure to the contribution of the United States of America. I am happy to take this occasion to express to you, the Congress which has approved this assistance, the sincere and lasting appreciation of my people.

This collaboration with the West and with the United States in particular has taken yet broader forms. There is our military collaboration based on Mutual Security program. If we leave out the Atlantic group, Ethiopia has been the only state of the Middle East to follow the example of the United States in sending forces to Korea for the defense of collective security.

In so doing, Ethiopia has been inspired by a vision which is broader than her preoccupation with regional policies or advantages. Nearly two decades ago, I personally assumed before history the responsibility of placing the fate of my beloved people on the issue of collective security, for surely, at that time and for the first time in world history, that issue was posed in all its clarity. My searching of conscience convinced me of the rightness of my course and if, after untold sufferings and, indeed, unaided resistance at the time of aggression, we now see the final vindication of that principle in our joint action in Korea, I can only be thankful that God gave me strength to persist in our faith until the moment of its recent glorious vindication.

We do not view this principle as an extenuation for failing to defend one's homeland to the last drop of one's blood, and, indeed, our own struggles during the last two decades bear testimony to our conviction that in matters of collective security as of Providence, God helps him who helps himself".

However, We feel that no where can the call for aid against aggression be refused by any state large or small. It is either a universal principle or it is no principle at all. It cannot admit of regional application or be of regional responsibility. That is why We, like you, have sent troops half-way around the world to Korea. We must face that responsibility for its application wherever it may arise in these troubled hours of world history. Faithful and to the sacred memory of her patriots who fell in Ethiopia and in Korea in defense of that principle, Ethiopia cannot do otherwise.

The world has ceaselessly sought for and striven to apply some system for assuring the peace of the world. Many solutions have been proposed and many have failed. Today the system which we have advocated and with which the name of Ethiopia is inseparably associated has, after her sacrifices of two decades ago, and her recent sacrifices with the United States and others in Korea, finally demonstrated its worth. However, no system, not even that of collective security, can succeed unless there is not only firm determination to apply it universally both in space and time, but at whatever be the cost. Having successfully applied the system of collective security in Korea, we must now, wherever in the world the peace is threatened, pursue its application more resolutely than ever and with courageous acceptance of its burdens. We have a sacred duty to our children to spare them the sacrifices which we have known. I call upon the world for determination fearlessly to apply and accept as you and as We have accepted them – the sacrifices of collective security.

It is here that our common Christian heritage unites two peoples across the globe in a community of ideals and endeavor. Ethiopia seeks only to apply and broaden that cooperation between peace-loving nations."

H.I.M. Haile Selassie addresses joint session of Congress

Later in the day, during a television interview on "Youth Want to Know" **His Imperial Majesty** said, *"Collective security is the basis of our foreign policy and Ethiopia is prepared to stand against aggression wherever it may appear. . . . Small nations can only preserve their independence by standing together."*

H.I.M also visited the National Cathedral that, as Regent of Ethiopia in the early 1920's, he presented with a gold cross. As Emperor, His Majesty made a second gift of a gold and silver censer.

Washington, D.C.: H.I.M. Haile Selassie I Emperor of Ethiopia toured Washington Episcopal Cathedral with Bishop Angus Dun as his guide. H.I.M. Haile Selassie I Emperor of Ethiopia greeted an American Boy Scout while on a tour of the Washington Episcopal Cathedral in the company of Bishop Angus Dun.

H.I.M. Emperor Haile Selassie I and Bishop Angus Dun leave the Washington Episcopal Cathedral after the special worship services held for the distinguished visitor from Ethiopia.

At a state dinner given by His Majesty at the Ethiopian Embassy in honor of President Eisenhower, the Emperor presented official Ethiopian decorations to President Eisenhower; Admiral Radford, Chairman of the Joint Chiefs of Staff; Mr. Harold Stassen, head of the Foreign Operations Administration; President Mordecai Johnson of Howard University; Mr. Henry Byroade, Assistant Secretary of State for the Near East and Africa; and the US Ambassador to Ethiopia, Dr. Joseph Simonson, who received the Grand Cordon of the Order of Star of Ethiopia.

The U.S. Library of Congress opened a special exhibit consisting of books, official documents, photographs of Ethiopia's historic buildings and monuments, its educational centers and highlights of its recent past, all honoring His Majesty's presence in the nation's capital. The exhibit was the first of its kind in the United States.

This large manuscript map of the Kingdom of Ethiopia once hung in the palace of His Royal Highness Ras Tafari, later known as Emperor Haile Selassie I. Presented to the Library in 1924 by Homer L. Shantz, who received it personally from Ras Tafari along with "some spears, shields, and coins" while on an official U.S. mission to map African vegetation, it was prepared by the court geographer in Addis Ababa "by order of the Regent" in 1923. His Imperial Majesty was reunited with the map when he viewed it during a visit to the Library of Congress on May 28, 1954, and recalled its presentation to Dr. Shantz thirty years earlier. (*Library of Congress Vault Map Collection*)

Saturday, May 29:

His Imperial Majesty visits Princeton University. Waiting for H.I.M on the steps of the Graduate School were the Dean of the faculty and Dean of the Graduate School. United States Senator Alexander Smith of New Jersey made a surprise visit to see His Majesty. While visiting the famous University library, His Majesty saw some ancient Ethiopian manuscripts on display. Among these were one of the Four Gospels written during the reign of King John in 1650, part of the Gospel of St. Luke written in Ge'ez in the sixteenth century and a seventeenth century book of the saints. There was also a letter written by the Emperor Menelik II in 1900.

One of America's Old Universities, Princeton, Acts as Host on Visit of His Imperial Majesty

PRINCETON, New Jersey, May 29 — Ending the first week of his American tour, Emperor Haile Selassie today visited historic Princeton University, founded in 1746.

On the steps of the Graduate School the Dean of the faculty and Dean of the Graduate School were waiting to greet the Emperor. With His Imperial Majesty at the head, the party then walked through the gray stone buildings that make up the many colleges of the University. They stopped at the Cleveland Bell Tower, named in honor of one of America's most famous presidents and other spots of interest.

Returning to their autos the Emperor's party drove to the University library, pausing on the way to view the home of the famous scientist, Albert Einstein, now a Professor at Princeton.

At this point of the tour, word had begun to spread about the campus that the Emperor was there, and the crowd following the Emperor became larger and more pressing.

At the library, the University displayed some of the Ethiopian documents from its famed Robert Garrett collection, named for the man who made a special educational expedition to Ethiopia in 1905-1906.

Among these items were a manuscript of the four Gospels written during the reign of King John in 1650; a portion of the Gospel of Luke, written in the ancient Coptic tongue of the sixth century; an illuminated 17th century book of saints; and several old Ethiopian Christian manuscripts.

Included also, were a letter penned by Emperor Menelik II, dated June 7, 1900 and many other later items of historical interest.

In the library the Emperor, Prince Sahle Selassie, and Princess Sebla Desta signed the library guest book.

A member of the library staff, Doctor Rice, explained the workings of the library's orrery which calculates movements of the planets. Dr. Rice spoke in French, which the Emperor seemed to enjoy. His Imperial Majesty demonstrated his mastery of this language by engaging in a light and rapid discourse with Dr. Rice.

The faculty of the University then held a reception for the Emperor in the faculty lounge. The Emperor personally greeted the faculty and other school officials, who lined up to shake his hand.

A surprise visitor was United States Senator Alexander Smith of New Jersey, who heard the Emperor was coming to Princeton and came to the University especially to see His Imperial Majesty.

After the ordeal of meeting hundreds of people, the Emperor bade the University "Goodbye" and his party resumed their trip to New York City by motorcade. State Police escorted the cars and passing through each town, local motorcycle police provided additional escort.

Ethiopian Herald no. 50 vol. 11 Saturday, June 5, 1954.

Ethiopian Herald No.50 Vol.11 Saturday June 5, 1954 courtesy of IES

Sunday, May 30:

His Imperial Majesty attends early morning services at the Hellenic Cathedral of the Holy Trinity, the Greek Orthodox Church. Archbishop Michael of the Greek Orthodox Church of North and South America chanted the liturgy while the Emperor occupied a place especially arranged for him at the front of the church. After the service, His Majesty presented a gold cross to the Archbishop for the Cathedral. H.I.M. visits Hyde Park, NY, home of former President Franklin D. Roosevelt. H.I.M. also visits the Abyssinian Baptist Church in Harlem. Hulan Jack, President of Manhattan greeted H.I.M. upon arrival, as well as throngs of crowds with Ethiopian flags.

New York: H.I.M. is introduced to Greek orthodox archbishop Michael after a solemn Doxology service in New York's Cathedral of the Holy Trinity. During the service, the Archbishop honored the visiting Emperor and praised his country, which, he said, faced with supreme heroism for years the vicious hordes of fascism.

Roosevelt Ancestral Estate at Hyde Park Visited And Paid Homage by The Emperor

NEW YORK, May 30. — Emperor Haile Selassie this morning visited Hyde Park, home of former President Franklin D. Roosevelt and now a national shrine.

Waiting at the entrance was Mrs. Roosevelt, widow of the President, who greeted His Imperial Majesty and conducted him to the tomb. Here, at the tomb of an American known and revered by many persons alive today, and by many now watching nearby, the Emperor laid a floral wreath. Turning to Mrs. Roosevelt and the crowd assembled a short distance away, the Emperor said: "As you know Mrs. Roosevelt, it is a little more than 10 years ago since your husband asked me to come to Hyde Park. I thanked him then, and I thank you now".

"I knew the statesman, the incomparable leader of not only his own but also so many nations. I feel today, Mrs. Roosevelt, I know more of the man."

Continuing the Emperor stated: "I shall not even try to express my admiration and my respect for President Roosevelt and I even hesitate to express my regard for your own great services to humanity and mankind."

Mrs. Roosevelt then thanked the Emperor for his kind gesture, congratulated him for leading his nation to such a respected place in the family of nations, and praised the record Ethiopian soldiers had carved for their country in the Korean war.

She said: "I have met many Ethiopians in the United States and abroad, and my respect and admiration for them is the highest".

The ex-president's widow then led the Emperor through the mansion showing him the rooms where he had studied and reached many of the decisions that were to influence history and pointing out the places where he relaxed and played with his family.

On display in the library of President Roosevelt are the gold of Africa sent to the former President by His Imperial Majesty, a huge photograph of their historic meeting aboard a warship in the Red Sea during World War II, an autographed picture of the Emperor, and Mr. Roosevelt's collection of Ethiopian stamps.

H.I.M. visits Hyde Park, NY, home of former President Franklin D. Roosevelt.

Hyde Park, New York: H.I.M. Haile Selassie and Mrs. Franklin D. Roosevelt after laying a wreath at the grave of the late President Roosevelt at Hyde Park, New York. Later in the day, Mrs. Roosevelt gave a luncheon in honor of the Emperor at the Roosevelt home.

Extremely Spontaneous Welcome Given to The Ethiopian Emperor by Huge Harlem Crowds

NEW YORK, May 30. — The most enthusiastic and spontaneous welcome Emperor Haile Selassie has received in the United States was accorded him this afternoon by the citizens in the Harlem section of New York.

The occasion was his visit to the Abyssinian Baptist Church built in 1898 by American citizens of African descent.

As his party reached the city boundary after returning from Hyde Park, Hulan Jack, President of Manhattan borough of two million people, was waiting to greet him.

As the Emperor's party neared the Church thousands of persons cheered loudly as his car passed. Hundreds of Ethiopian flags were waved, in the Church, the service was led by Rev. Adam Clayton Powell, also a representative in the Congress. During the service Rev. Powell described His Imperial Majesty as one who had meant much to Americans of African descent because of his leadership in demonstrating the key role that developing nations of that continent could play in world history.

Emperor Haile Selassie of Ethiopia today inspected colour television

H.I.M. Haile Sellasie I also visited the Abyssinian Baptist Church in New York and presented an Ethiopian Gold Processional Crown to the Reverend Adam Clayton Powell.

Hulan Jack, President of Manhattan greeted H.I.M. upon arrival, as well as large crowds of people with Ethiopian flags

Editorial

EMPEROR CONTINUES TO MAKE WORLD HISTORY

His Imperial Majesty's visit to the United States is itself historic. This could be gleaned from the type of reception and admiration accorded the Emperor in his sojourn in that country. The sentiments expressed on [...]

THE ETHIOPIAN HERALD

Collective Security Declared Vital in Ethiopia's Interest

WASHINGTON, May 27. — Experience has taught Ethiopia that collective security against aggression is vital for small nations, Ethiopian Emperor Haile Selassie declared today.

"We are convinced and nothing will divert us from this conviction, that collective security can alone be the answer for the future," the visiting Monarch said in an address at a luncheon sponsored by a joint press and radio committee.

"We fence and maintain", he pointed [...] conviction confirmed [...] but also to [...] by he achieved by [...]

[...] in 1936 to gain [...] League of Nations [...] been vindicated [...] in Korea the [...] expressed pride in [...] U.N. and other UN [...] defending the [...]

The Emperor described Ethiopia's progress in the last decade as "unprecedented". He pointed out that in this period, "imports and exports have quadrupled, as have our holdings doubled over those of the previous year. Our national budget has doubled as has the amount of currency in circulation. The costs of our national bank have, since the liberation, increased 20 times over. We have no national debt, except for two development loans from the International Bank for improvement of highways and telecommunications."

This great progress, he said, is due in part to American assistance and support. I would be happy indeed if my great country would serve [...] inducing more engineers, [...] American capital to come [...] added.

[...] spent most of today [...] tour in the Washington [...] the tomb of George [...] first U.S. President.

Emperor Issues Statement To United Nations Correspondets

U. N. HEADQUARTERS. — In a statement to United Nations correspondents on the occasion of his visit to the United Nations headquarters, His Majesty Haile Selassie, the Emperor of Ethiopia said:

U.N. Headquarters Paid Visit by The Emperor

NEW YORK, June 2. — Emperor Haile Selassie of Ethiopia yesterday afternoon paid his first visit to United Nations headquarters here.

THE ETHIOPIAN HERALD

City Of New York Honors The Emperor With Big Luncheon

NEW YORK. — At a luncheon given by the City of New York in honor of Emperor Haile Selassie of Ethiopia at Waldorf Astoria Hotel.

United Nations Secretary General Gives Dinner in Honor of Emperor

Emperor Haile Selassie Faces Barrage Of Questions at New York Press Conference

NEW YORK, June 1. — Emperor Haile Selassie of Ethiopia this morning faced the questions of reporters in a typical American press Conference. There was no advance knowledge of what the newsmen would ask. Reporters were called upon to ask questions in the order in which they raised their hands.

Tuesday, June 1: At ceremonies for His Imperial Majesty at City Hall at noon, **Hulan Jack , Borough President of Manhattan**, made the following address: "Your Imperial Majesty, Haile Selassie, Emperor of Ethiopia, Your Imperial Highness Prince Sahle Selassie, Your Imperial Highness Princess Sebla Desta, Mayor Wagner, Ambassador Patterson, distinguished guests, ladies and gentleman: For many, many years, the people of the United States have warmly admired the inspiring courage which Your Imperial Majesty symbolized during the struggles of Ethiopia, a nation rich in culture, with a continuous history of 3,000 years. As the titular head of the Ethiopian Church and the 'Defender of the Faith," the Christian principles of brotherhood expressed by Your Imperial Majesty has the respect of the people of those United States who have dedicated ourselves to the protection of liberty, justice and human rights. As Your Imperial Majesty travels through the wonderland of America during the next few weeks, I am sure its magic spell of industry and vision will endear us to the hearts and minds of the people of Ethiopia, thereby cementing further our lasting friendship . . . . "

At a New York Press Conference, a woman reporter asked him what he thought of the recent United States Supreme Court decision outlawing racial segregation in the public schools of some states. **His Imperial Majesty** replied, *"This historic court decision resting on your Constitution will win the esteem of the entire world for the United States. And in particular it will win the esteem of all the colored people of the world."*

Mayor Robert Wagner, city officials, and leading citizens of New York give a luncheon at the Waldorf-Astoria Hotel for Emperor Haile Selassie. Welcoming His Imperial Majesty on behalf of 8 million New York citizens, **Mayor Wagner** stated, "My good friends: we pay honour today to a very great man, a man who represents one of the most ancient governments and cultures in the world and who, with progressive thinking and constructive planning, has brought his nation to the forefront of modern civilization. The heritage and tradition of 3,000 years of royal lineage encouraged our most distinguished guest of honor to ever greater efforts on behalf of his people and thereby to enormous contributions to the welfare of the world. We honor today an Emperor, a King, the royal leader of a royal country. But His Imperial Majesty, Haile Selassie I, more than Emperor, more than a King, proved himself to be a man, a great man with courage; with vision; with determination; with humanity; and with humility. He gave his ancient nation its first written constitution, relinquishing much of his authority to a Parliament and a judicial system, thereby encouraging the greater development of democracy in his country. He developed health services, hospitals, schools, a broader education system and lent tremendous encouragement to the recruitment of doctors, nurses, engineers and teachers. His has been a life of understanding and tolerance and his is the mark of true greatness. During the course of his historic visit to our country he will visit many cities. And I venture to say with great pride that he will find in this city—our city—the warmth, the enthusiasm and the wholehearted welcome of all of our eight million people.

He will find here in New York that we live in accordance with the highest aspiration of the United Nations which is headquartered here. We live in peace and in unity. Your Imperial Majesty, may I say, on behalf of all the people of my city, that we are most happy and most proud to have you with us. You typify that in which we believe. You share with us faith in the United Nations and hatred for totalitarian aggression, your people fought with our people in Korea and your country and ours have exchanged diplomatic missions for the past fifty years. You strive for the same social progress as we do and the contributions of your country through the centuries to the welfare of America have been manifold—incalculable. We are glad you are here. We know that your visit will result in greater mutual understanding, respect and admiration between our respective peoples. You symbolize the decency and the morality of your country. We think you will find that New York City likewise symbolizes the decency and morality of the United States. Welcome, Sir, and God bless you."

United Nations Secretary General Dag Hammarskjold also welcomed the Emperor, stating, "I am deeply conscious of the honour you have accorded me in inviting me to participate in this welcome to Your Imperial Majesty, Emperor Haile Selassie of Ethiopia. . . . The Emperor of Ethiopia stands in the perspective of the history of our time as a symbolic landmark, A PROPHETIC FIGURE of the path of man's struggle to achieve international peace and security through concerted international action. I recall the eloquent address Your Majesty delivered before the Assembly of the League of Nations in 1936. Your Majesty then said . . . .'It is international morality that is at stake and not the articles of the covenant" . . . . Your Majesty and the people of Ethiopia demonstrated this will to fulfill international undertakings in response to a resolution of the UN Security Council of 27 June 1950. A contingent of Ethiopian troops joined the armed forces of other members of the UN Under the Unified Command in Korea. They traveled from one end of the world to the other to offer their lives in a remote area where Ethiopia had no conceivable national interest, save that of vindicating a principle."

H.I.M. Haile Selassie I and entourage in front of the United Nations

The Emperor then made his first visit to the United Nations headquarters in New York. In a statement to the United Nations correspondents, **His Majesty** said, *"Ever since my country's acceptance of the obligations of the United Nations as a charter member, I have looked forward to the day when I would be able to visit the organization's headquarters. The physical realization in these splendid buildings, of the hopes and aspirations of those of us who have ardently supported the principle of collective security and the practical instruments to secure and maintain international justice has surpassed my expectation. I have enjoyed meeting our able Secretary General and members of his staff, but I am not less conscious of the important and conscientious service rendered to the organization by the press corps. You are quite literally the eyes and ears of the United Nations and it is through you that the world can follow and can judge the realization of their faith in the United Nations. I have always been grateful to the press for their awareness of the importance of the principle of collective security and of my efforts to establish that principle in effective action. I am confident that within the scope of your dedicated task of objectively reporting the achievements of the organization you will never fail to reflect the patient faith of all peoples that ONLY THROUGH DISCUSSION, COLLABORATION, AGREEMENT AND ENFORCEMENT OF THE WILL OF MANKIND CAN WORLD PEACE AND STABILITY BE ACHIEVED."*

At a dinner given in His Honor by the UN General Secretary, **His Imperial Majesty Haile Selassie** says,

"It is a significant moment for me, when, after eighteen years, I again find myself in a center where are concentrated the passionate hopes of the thousands of millions of human beings who so desperately long for the assurance of peace. The years of that interval, somber as they were and sacred as they remain to the memory of millions of innocent victims, hold forth for us bright hope of the future. The League of Nations failed and failed basically because of its inability to prevent aggression against my country. But, neither the depth of that failure nor the intervening catastrophes could dull the perception of the need and the search for peace through collective security. So it is that here in the United Nations we have dedicated ourselves anew to those high and indeed essential ideals, essential if the world is to continue on the path of peace. Ethiopia, for its part, is profoundly convinced of the triumph of these ideals, were it only that the past two decades have, in her case, fully justified them. The League of Nations may have failed, but Ethiopia was again liberated and through the United Nations has finally seen the rectification of seventy years of injustice and the vindication of the right of brothers to become reunited. Moreover, the memory of the failure two decades ago of measures of collective security is being effaced by the glorious achievement, to which Ethiopia also contributed, in the collective defense of Korea. Surely we have cause to be heartened at the progress of mankind. We must lay aside any disappointment of the hour lest it cloud our vision of the goal to which we would attain and press forward, with confidence, born of past experience, in the triumph of principles which are here represented and for which you, Mr. Secretary-General, labor so diligently and intelligently."

Wednesday, June 2:

Emperor Haile Selassie visits New York's radio center, views color television for the first time, and watches a Connecticut couple get married. With Laurence Rockefeller as an escort, H.I.M. visits 65th floor of the Radio Corporation of America. H.I.M then heads to City Hall and awards New York Mayor Robert Wagner the Grand Cordon of the Order of Menelik, the highest civilian decoration awarded by Ethiopia. He also presented the Mayor with two joined elephant tusks, a red and gold shield, and two silver-tipped spears.

His Imperial Majesty was presented with a scroll by New York Mayor Robert F. Wagner. On the scroll were the words,

"Our people have a long and profound admiration for you and your gallant country. We have been impressed with your gentleness, your culture, your passion for progress and your character as a great leader of a magnificent and ancient nation."

At Columbia University, where His Imperial Majesty's two grandsons, Merid and Samson, are students, H.I.M was presented with an Honorary Doctor of Laws Degree. In accepting the Degree, the **Emperor** said, *"Throughout my long reign, I have always been preoccupied with the importance of the educational development of my nation. More of our resources have gone into education than into any other social or governmental activity. We have solicited and are accepting technical assistance from abroad, and in particular, from the United States, in this all-important function because history has shown not only that in the letters is to be found the truth, but also that no country can operate in the world without a corps of professionally educated elite of its own nationals."*

New York City: HIM is awarded an honorary Doctor of Laws Degree by Colombia University's President Grayson Kirk. Dr. Philip Jessup, Professor of International Law stands to the Emperor's left. After receiving the degree, the Emperor said, *"it is a signal honor for me to accept, in token efforts in the field of education, this award from so distinguished an institution of learning."*

At the Council of Foreign Relations, His Imperial Majesty said, *"The chief of Government of a small but supremely courageous state on the eve of the outbreak of the first World War declared that one of the most difficult tasks in the world was to conduct the foreign affairs of a small country. Surely, this observation applies today no less than forty years ago. For a small state, foreign policy is the very basis of its existence since power alone can never suffice to that end. Every small state, in the final analysis, is driven to make decisions after the most searching reflections. Indeed, today, one is compelled to inquire whether there is sufficient assurance for the continued existence of small states. For our part, we do not share this feeling of pessimism, although conditions of the present hour make the struggle for existence an exceedingly difficult one. We feel it important that small states should be able to survive and make their contribution to the maintenance of world peace. Small states bring to bear an element of tolerance and comprehension that would otherwise be lacking to a great extent in the world today. This is clearly the case in Ethiopia. It is not surprising, therefore, that history confirms the conclusion that compromise settlements most often proceed from small states. This is the case with the work of the United Nations where, the compromise formulate that have been carried into execution, have frequently been those proposed not by a large state or states, but rather by the smaller members or groups of members of the United Nations. Finally, it is certain that the basic support of the principle of collective security, comes, less from the larger states, than from the small states which have more to gain and more to lose by failure in its application. In this respect, it is significant that the smaller states associated in the United Nations efforts in Korea outnumbered the larger states. If, then, it is important that small states continue to make their contribution to world peace, and if, on the other hand, the development of power politics would seem to threaten their very existence, how can this dilemma be faced? In the past, there have been several possible solutions to this problem. The system of alliances was, of course, one alternative that has been followed in the past. However, the first world war threatened this solution and the events immediately preceding the outbreaking of the second World War weakened it still further. Another possibility was one based upon the strategic importance of small states. The natural consequences of this fact was for such states either to adopt a forthright and immutable policy of neutrality or, contrariwise, to adopt the policy of playing off one group against the other. Although for Ethiopia a policy of neutrality has long been attractive were it only for reasons of geographical isolation, her traditions exclude such a choice, and, indeed, the conditions of the modern world render such a policy difficult of execution for any small state. On the other hand, Ethiopia abhors a policy of simultaneously seeking advantages from opposing factions and events of recent months elsewhere in the world have shown that where such a policy is being followed, it is of no results. Even where results are to be obtained, it is extremely doubtful whether, with the outbreak of war, they could serve to assure the neutrality or independence of any such state. Finally, there was, and there still is formally, at least, the system of regional defenses and pacts. For its part, at the Conference of San Francisco which drafted the Charter of the United Nations, Ethiopia was alone to point out the pitfalls of this solution. There are, of course, regional agreements in force in certain restricted areas of the world—the North Atlantic Treaty Organization and European Defense Community are so vast as to fall outside this restriction—but present-day events show only too clearly that broader solutions are required and that regionalism, in the final analysis does a disservice to the principle of collective security. Ethiopia is profoundly convinced that collective security can alone afford the answer to this problem and that it must be recognized as having not regional but universal validity. Otherwise its deterrent as well as its defensive effect will be of manifestly insufficient force. It was in support of this conviction that Ethiopia was one of the first of the United Nations and the only one from the Middle East to join the appeal for the collective defense of Korea, half-way around the world from Africa. Such are the problems with which a small country, such as Ethiopia, is faced. No small country can hope to effect a rational decision which, in the end, will serve to assure its independence, when that decision is based on a balancing out of factors, for today no such balancing out can any longer be achieved. We can only make our choice and, to adopt an American phrase, to stand up and be counted."*

His Imperial Majesty visits Boston and at a luncheon, **H.I.M.** said the people of other nations are *"often impressed rather with the material strength of the United States. Here in Boston we have the opportunity of visiting what is undoubtedly the cultural capital of the United States. We have been tremendously impressed with the wealth of learning amassed around the city of Boston in institutions of unparalleled influence."* His Majesty then departed for Ottawa.

Thursday, June 3: H.I.M arrives in Ottawa, Canada aboard a Royal Canadian Air Force plane departing from Boston. Governor-General Vincent Massey and Prime Minister St. Laurent headed a reception party for the Emperor as artillery thundered out the 21-gun salute.

Saturday, June 5: Governor-General Vincent Massey gives grand reception in honor of His Imperial Majesty. Present as guests were Canadian Ministers, members of the Diplomatic Corps, and high-ranking Canadian personalities. H.I.M visits Canadian Parliament and the President of the Parliament said, "His Imperial Majesty is a living symbol of justice and right and a source of inspiration to all men who love freedom. He personifies the sacred principles of international harmony based on collective security."

In Montreal, McGill University awards His Majesty with an Honorary Degree. Afterwards, His Imperial Majesty proceeded to Quebec aboard the steamer "Iberville" on the Saint Lawrence River. Laval University in Quebec awarded His Majesty an Honorary Degree. The Lieutenant-Governor of Quebec gave a luncheon party in honor of His Imperial Majesty. As H.I.M. passed through the streets of Quebec, people in the crowded streets applauded. All Canadian newspapers and radio and television stations gave details of H.I.M. biography and Ethiopia's history.

Sunday, June 6: His Imperial Majesty spends the night in Windsor, Ontario

Ethiopian Herald No. 51 Vol. 11 Saturday, June 12, 1954 courtesy of IES

Monday, June 7: H.I.M. motorcades through Detroit, Michigan and arrives in Ann Arbor at 10:30 a.m. where His Majesty received an Honorary Doctor of Civil Law Degree from the University of Michigan. **University Vice-President Marvin L. Niehuss** said that, "His Imperial Majesty reflects the enviable characteristics of his earliest forbearer— sagacity and great courage" and called H.I.M.'s doctrine of collective security an "enduring monument of history."

H.I.M. departs from Lansing, Michigan by plane and arrives in Chicago. Police estimated that 59,000 people lined the route that his police-escorted motorcade took from the airport to the Drake Hotel.

Cicero, Illinois: H.I.M. Haile Selassie I Emperor of Ethiopia (left) and his grand daughter Princess Seble Desta (right) were welcomed on their arrival in Chicago by Mayor Martin Kennelly (Second from right). The Princess receives flowers from airline stewards Barbara LeVack. The Emperor and his party visited Chicago's industry as part of his US tour.

Tuesday, June 8: Chicago Mayor Martin Kennelly headed the city's official welcome to the Emperor and stated, "He is a world figure who symbolizes lion-hearted courage and passionate resistance to aggression and enslavement. In his leadership and example, he stands for the progress of his nation, the prosperity and security of his people and the peace of the world."

Chicago, IL: H.I.M. presents Chicago's Mayor Martin H. Kennelly with a medal, symbol of the Grand Office of the Order of the Star of Ethiopia. The Emperor has conferred this special honor on several important officials during his tour of the U.S.

Cicero, Illinois H.I.M. Haile Selassie I Emperor of Ethiopia and his official party visit the Burlington Clyde diesel shop and roundhouse in Cicero, Illinois. Mr. H.H. Urbach, (left) Assistant Vice President of the Burlington railroads, acts as guide. Here His Imperial Majesty tries his hand at operating a machine. The Emperor, who is on a good will tour of the United States, is greeted by Cowboy Cliff Messoulz of Montana as He visited the Chicago Stockyards.

His Imperial Majesty arose at 6:00 a.m. in his Drake Hotel suite. After morning prayers and breakfasting on two eggs and milk, he refused the Drake Hotel's Royal Red Carpet and instead, exited out a side entrance and toured the Burlington railroad diesel shops and roundhouse in suburban Cicero, then the Swift Company meat packing plant and attended a civic luncheon where **His Majesty** told 1,000 of Chicago's top business, civic, and government leaders, *"Unlimited opportunities exist (in Ethiopia) for American capital and pioneering spirit in the development of the coffee industry, meat packing and shipping, tanning, and leather and shoe industries, tobacco and sugar. American business has the added protection not only of a recent commercial treaty, but what is equally important, an American dollar-based currency in Ethiopia. You can therefore freely bring back the profits of your investments."*

After the luncheon, the Imperial party visited a United States Steel Corporation plant and then made an unscheduled visit to Chicago's South side where His Majesty addressed 3,000 people at the South Park Baptist Church.

His Imperial Majesty Tours Rich Farming Region in Minnesota

ROCHESTER, MINNESOTA. — Silos jutting up from barnyards in Southern Minnesota were curiosities to Ethiopian Emperor Haile Selassie as he drove through the rolling countryside today. The Monarch had many questions about the silos (big metal and wooden storage bins) that are not used in his country.

Dr. Joseph Simonson, United States Ambassador to Ethiopia, said the Emperor had more questions about the Silos than about machinery or crops during the 90-mile trip from St. Paul and Minneapolis to the Edwin Doty farm near here.

Tonight Haile Selassie was guest at a dinner on the University of Minnesota Campus in Minneapolis. The National Students Nurses Association presented him with books on nursing education to be placed in the Princess Tsahai Memorial Hospital. The Princess, daughter of the Emperor, was a nurse.

Wednesday, June 9:

His Imperial Majesty visits Minnesota. At the University of Minnesota Campus in Minneapolis, the National Students Nurses Association presented H.I.M. with books on nursing education to be placed in the Princess Tsahai Memorial Hospital. Dr. Joseph Simonson, United States Ambassador to Ethiopia, accompanied H.I.M on the 90-mile trip from St. Paul to the Edwin Doty farm where the Emperor took great interest in the many storage silos spread through the rolling countryside. H.I.M. also visits the University of Minnesota Agricultural campus and the famous Mayo clinic.

St. Paul, Minnesota: H.I.M. rides in a parade through the streets of St. Paul with the emperor are Minnesota's governor C. Elmer Anderson back seat and state Adjutant General Joseph Nelson.

St. Paul Minnesota: H.I.M. Emperor Haile Selassie I Emperor of Ethiopia presents a gold and silver cross and to the reverend M.A. Egge, pastor of Christ Lutheran Church in St. Paul.

THE ETHIOPIAN HERALD

No. 52 - Vol. 11
Saturday, June 19, 1954.

A WEEKLY NEWSPAPER
PUBLISHED IN ADDIS ABABA

Subscription Rates (postage included): In Ethiopia:
— 1 year: Eth.$ 6.24 — Six Months: Eth.$ 3.12
— Foreign (postage included) 1 year: Eth.$ 9.50

PRICE
Eth. 12 Cents

Ethiopian Emperor Makes Extensive Tour Of American Northwest and Pacific Coast; Given Big Civic Welcome in San Francisco

His Imperial Majesty is here seen on His visit to Mt. Vernon, ancestral home of George Washington, first American President

His Imperial Majesty is here seen with United Nations Secretary-General Dag Hammarskjold. Centre is H.E. The Ethiopian Foreign Minister, Ato Aklilou Habtewold

Tomb of the American Unknown Soldier in Arlington Cemetery is visited by His Imperial Majesty

American Girls' School Paid Visit by Princess Tenagne Work

HER IMPERIAL HIGHNESS INSPECTS WORK AND IS ENTERTAINED

Her Imperial Highness Princess Tenagne Work visited the American Mission Girls' School, Gulellei, on Saturday morning, June 5. The pupils of the school lined the driveway to welcome her. Her Imperial Highness was greeted by Miss Ruth M. Nichol, the Directress of the school and by Miss E. E. McCreery, the acting Directress during the

B-U-L-L-E-T-I-N

YOSEMITE NATIONAL PARK, California, June 16 - The Nation's first and most famous National Park last night was host to the reigning Monarch of the oldest Christian nation in the world. Haile Selassie viewed the glacier-made wonders of Yosemite Valley yesterday afternoon, after his busy one-day visit to San Francisco. The spectacular mountain region lies between San Francisco and Los Angeles, his next stop, and is on the western slope of the Sierra Nevada mountains.

The park has 752,744 acres of mountains and forests, 429 lakes, a chain of mountain peaks averaging 10,000 feet or more, and five great water-falls. The valley itself is rough seven miles long, with an average width of

Ethiopian Parliament Adjourns Members Leave on Recess;

HIS IMPERIAL HIGHNESS THE CROWN PRINCE ADDRESSES MEMBERS

Members of the Chamber of Deputies, led by His Excellency Blatta Zawde Belcineh, President of the Chamber, were received by His Imperial Highness the Crown Prince at the Imperial Palace Thursday at 11 a.m. The Parliament, as customary, has recessed and its the absence of His Majesty the Emperor, the deputies were at the Imperial Palace to pay their homage and to take leave of the Crown before going on furlough.

Addressing H. I. H. the Crown Prince, the Member for Wollo said

His Imperial Majesty flies from Minneapolis to Spokane, Washington and visits the Grand Coulee Dam, the largest in the world. H.I.M. was very interested in the multi-purpose hydro-electric project because Ethiopia has the potential of a large scale water power development.

Top left: His Imperial Majesty inspects Honour Guard at the Bremerton Naval Base in Washington. Top right: H.I.M. on the docks at Bremerton Naval Base. Bottom left and right HIM inspects workshops at Bremerton Naval Base.

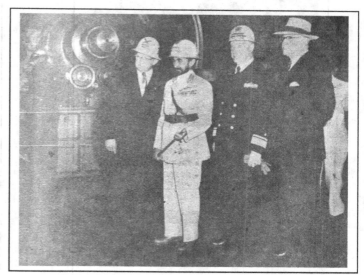

His Imperial Majesty in Seattle: During H.I.M.'s tour of the Pacific coastal states, H.I.M. saw the Boeing airplane plant and visited the United States Army's Seattle Port of embarkation.

H.I.M. (pictured with Princess Sebla Desta) arrives in Seattle at the Port on Lake Washington. His Imperial Majesty's entourage stayed at the Olympic Hotel. There was a reception sponsored by the Rainier Club and they inspected the Boeing plant.

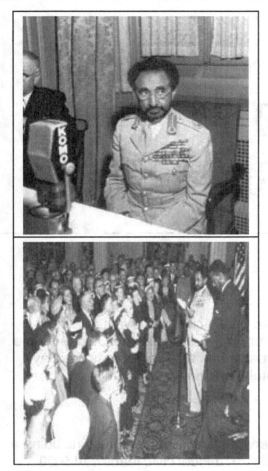

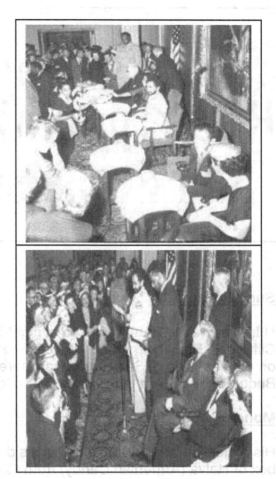

Pictures above and on the previous page are courtesy of The Ethiopian World Federation Emperor Yekuno Amlak Local No. 16 exhibit in commemoration of the 47th anniversary of the visit of Emperor Haile Selassie I to the City of Seattle in 1954. Photos are from the Seattle Post Intelligencer Collection Museum of History & Industry.

During a tour of Boeing Air plane companies in Seattle H.I.M. is presented with a model of a Boeing B-52 by Boeing President William M. Allen. Seattle's Mayor Allan Pomeroy looks on. At the Emperor's right are his grand daughter Princess Sebla Desta and Prince Sahle Selassie. Photos courtesy of IES.

His Imperial Majesty Visits San Francisco on His Tour

Sunday, June 13:

H.I.M. arrives in San Francisco at night by train from the Pacific Northwest. Mayor Clifford E. Rishel turned out to welcome the Emperor on his arrival at the Oakland Mole on the east side of San Francisco where the royal party was whisked across the Bay Bridge by limousine to the Imperial Suite at the Hotel Mark Hopkins.

Monday, June 14:

His Majesty arose at 6:00 a.m. for his devotional services and received gifts, including a box of Halva (Armenian Candy) from George Mardikian, a local civic leader. At 9:00 a.m. he attended a Press Conference in His suite. Asked about the possibilities of a third World War, the **Emperor** said, *"Is it right that you are asking if another war is coming, when all nations are preparing for war? But, the strength of the United States will be a preventative of war."* Asked about the recent U.S. Supreme Court decision outlawing racial segregation in public schools in the south, the **Emperor** answered, *"That is no new thing in American thinking. The decision will not only strengthen the ties between Ethiopia and the United States, but will also win friends everywhere in the world."* **His Imperial Majesty** said the big nations of the free world could best combat the spread of Communism *"by giving economic help to small nations."*

At 10:00 a.m. the interview was ended and the Royal party traveled by limousine to the Fort Riley Veteran's Hospital on the western edge of the city to visit American soldiers wounded in Korea. The **Emperor** passed slowly through the wards, stopping at each bed to wish the soldiers *"good luck"* in English. He made a brief speech in Amharic reminding the veterans that Ethiopian soldiers had fought at their sides in the Korean conflict *"for liberty and justice and peace."*

His Majesty presented a huge silver and gold cross of the Ethiopian Orthodox Church to Dr. James G. Donnelly, Manager of the Hospital. Precisely at 11:45 a.m. the Emperor and his party arrived at San Francisco City Hall where he was greeted by Mayor Elmer Robinson.

The Mayor presented the Emperor with a Steuben Glass Goblet "to toast the peace" and a gavel made of redwood. In return, the Emperor presented the Mayor with two Elephant tusks, tipped with gold and mounted on a polished wooden base. From the City Hall, the Emperor was escorted to the Palace Hotel down Market Street in an open touring car. Thousands of San Franciscans lined the sidewalk. At the Palace Hotel, many of the state's leading citizens were waiting. Governor Goodwin Knight and Mayor Robinson made brief speeches of welcome.

Said **Mayor Robinson**, "We are proud and grateful for the courage of your Majesty and your brave people. The Christian world owes you a great debt. You have taught us that actions, not just words, are required to achieve for us that great goal of human solidarity, based on international justice and equity." In his speech, the **Emperor** paid tribute to the American flag, *"a flag known and honoured throughout the world."* He compared Ethiopia to California in agriculture and climate and added, *"minerals like those found in California, such as oil and gold, are to be had in Ethiopia and it is our hope to be able to utilize the same methods employed here."*

The Emperor received more civic dignitaries in his suite in the afternoon, and at 5:30 p.m. attended a reception at the Hotel given by the World Affairs Council of Northern California. **Dr. Henry Grady, former U.S. Ambassador to Greece and Iran**, introduced His Majesty to 400 people present as "a proven World Leader who spoke out for the rights of the small countries."

Pictured above: San Francisco, California – at official welcoming ceremonies in City Hall H.I.M. and San Francisco Mayor Elmer E. Robinson shake hands through gold tipped elephant tusks which the Emperor presented to the Mayor Robinson. The Mayor gave His Imperial Majesty in return a beautiful Steuben Glass Goblet.

After the reception, the Royal party attended a banquet at a Press and Union League Club, where a bronze bust of the Emperor, made by a noted local sculptor, Spero Anargyros, who sketched and photographed the Emperor while serving in Eritrea with the U.K. army during World War II, was unveiled. The **Emperor** said that Ethiopia was developing at an *"almost explosive"* rate. *"Technical experts sent by the American government are doing wonders in increasing our Agricultural Production. Other Americans are helping to prospect for oil and gold and are aiding in developing Ethiopia's outstandingly successful program of aviation."*

San Francisco; California – H.I.M. confers the Knight Grand cross of the order of the order of Ethiopia upon California Governor Goodwin Knight

Tuesday, June 15:

His Imperial Majesty departs at 8:00 a.m. for Southern California visiting Yosemite National Park along the way and spends the night. **H.I.M.** said, *"This is an extremely beautiful place. It reminds me of wooded regions in the southern part of my country, although this, of course, is much more spectacular."*

In Los Angeles, the Emperor toured the movie studios, had luncheon with one thousand persons, a sight-seeing drive through the movie-land homes of Beverly Hills and Belair, inspections of Long Beach Harbour and a look at Southern California's newest oil refinery. The Emperor traveled at the head of a block-long caravan of automobiles escorted by a squad of police motorcycle officers. At City Hall, troops from Fort MacArthur formed a smart color guard on either side of the steps. A second color guard of the American Legion, America's largest veteran's organization, stood at the entrance and the Los Angeles police band struck up the national anthem of Ethiopia as the Emperor was escorted to the platform. 3,000 spectators crowded the welcoming ceremony. H.I.M then toured 20th Century Fox Film Studios where he was shown a 19th century set and met some of the actors, including Marlon Brando, who was outfitted for the role of Napoleon. H.I.M. saw the equipment, the actors, the directors and the sets, all of which together create the American film industry.

I.N.P.-FOTO

H.I.M. Haile Selassie with Mr. Eloi Omar, General Manager of the Port of Long Beach, California.

Friday, June 18:

H.I.M arrives in Stillwater, Oklahoma. The royal party flew from Ontario, California, International Airport to Stillwater aboard the special Trans-World Airline Super Constellation, "Star of Bombay," a four-engined prop plane considered the top airliner at the time. The California-to-Oklahoma flight took about four hours, but the pilot, Captain V.J. Stott, at the Emperor's request, had circled over Grand Canyon and Hoover Dam for twenty minutes.   At 3:30 p.m., the Star of Bombay landed at Stillwater's Municipal Airport, where a crowd of 1,100 including national, state, and local dignitaries was on hand to greet the Emperor. It was a hot late Spring day with the temperature near 100 degrees, and many women carried parasols. The Stars and Stripes and the green, gold, and red banner of Ethiopia hung from two new flag poles erected for the occasion at the Searcy Field airport. As the A&M band played, Haile Selassie I, who stood five feet four inches tall, emerged from the plane dressed in a field marshall's sun tan dress uniform with nine rows of campaign ribbons (including the U.S. Legion of Merit) and carrying a very long leather swagger stick. His Imperial Majesty (as protocol required the Emperor to be called) gave a smart salute to his audience before being officially welcomed by President Willham, Stillwater's Mayor A.B. Alcott, Oklahoma Lieutenant Governor James E. Barry, and Ambassador Simonson. The Emperor had requested an opportunity to see "an Indian," and Acee Blue Eagle, a well- known Native American artist from Okmulgee, in full headdress and buckskin clothing, presented Selassie with a war bonnet and gave him the name "Great Buffalo High Chief."

Reporters from Tulsa and Oklahoma City radio and television stations were on hand to broadcast brief remarks by the Emperor (translated from Amharic, the official language of Ethiopia, by "tall fine-featured" Endalkatchew). To questions from newsmen, Haile Selassie said he was "greatly impressed by the overwhelming welcome" he had received in the United States "and by the variety of industry and the standard of living." He said he intended to tell his people about the United States in detail.

Some seventeen A&M deans, professors, and administrative officials and their wives had been assigned as escorts for the visitors. They shepherded the royal party into convertibles provided by a local automobile dealer for the occasion and traveled to the A&M campus in a parade of Buicks (the leather car seats were quite hot because the autos had been sitting for an hour in direct sunlight). The guests took a quick tour of the library and classroom building, where they were shown original blue-prints of the proposed Imperial Agricultural College, before going to their rooms at the "fashionable Student Union hotel."

The Emperor and his entourage stayed in the Presidential Suite, the entire third floor of the hotel. A snack bar was set up for the visitors on the fourth floor, and the Emperor's son, Sahle, had a jukebox in his room, where he enjoyed listening to records of Frank Sinatra and other "swoon crooners." Prince Sahle also showed a fondness for the Union's special-deluxe hot dogs and ice cream sundaes.

THE DINNER AND RECEPTION

At 6:00 p.m., 300 guests were invited to a formal dinner in Parlors A, B, and C of the Student Union that had been festooned with Ethiopian, U.S. and Oklahoma flags. The invitation list was a "who's who" of the Oklahoma power elite of the time. Among the guests were U.S. Senator Robert S. Kerr, Representative Carl Albert (D-OK) and other Congressmen, Governor Johnston E. Murray (whose term as Governor was coming to an end), Lieutenant Governor James E. Barry, state legislators, mayors of six Oklahoma cities, the Board of Regents for Oklahoma A&M College and the Oklahoma State Regents for Higher Education, sixteen college and university presidents, A&M administrators, faculty, students, alumni, and business leaders and ministers from Stillwater. Extra security guards were posted around the union building to protect the royal family and to help direct guests to their proper destinations.

The dinner guests were seated promptly at 6:00 p.m., but the head table remained empty. Someone announced over the public address system that "When the guest of honor enters the room, will everyone please stand." All of the head table dignitaries except the Emperor were gathered in a nearby lounge. No one knew why Selassie was delayed.

After thirty minutes, Abe Hesser, Director of the Student Union at the time, stepped out of the dining room to find the Emperor, only to be met by Haile Selassie, who had not been feeling well, coming down the hall. Hesser barely had time to re-enter the banquet hall and shout "His Majesty, the King!" bringing the guests to their feet. Ambassador Simonson led the head table procession into the room with the Emperor entering last to take his seat between Willham and Governor Murray's wife, Willie (who had just launched the first attempt by a woman to seek the Democratic Party's gubernatorial nomination). William J. Hage, minister of Stillwater's First Presbyterian Church (where Willham attended), gave an invocation, and the diners feasted on a five course dinner featuring baked tenderloin with mushroom sauce and other delicacies prepared by the Union's building chefs.

In his after-dinner welcoming speech, Governor Murray praised Haile Selassie as "a symbol of the spark of freedom." President Willham presented His Imperial Majesty with a scroll expressing respect and sincere admiration. A&M's Vice President and Dean of Agriculture, Dr. Al E. Darlow, gave the Emperor a bronze plaque, given "on behalf of the citizens of Oklahoma," commemorating A&M's successful program of technical assistance and economic cooperation. The plaque read:

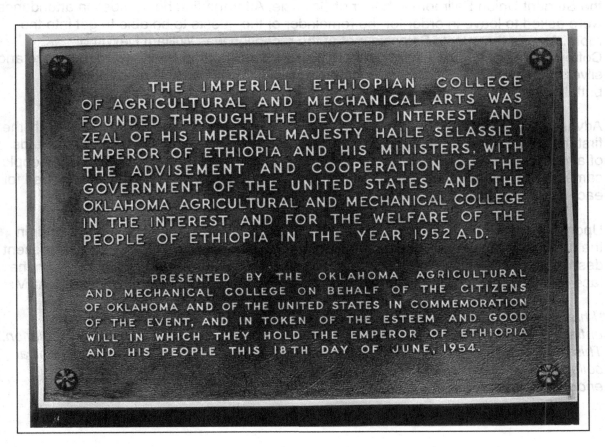

THE IMPERIAL ETHIOPIAN COLLEGE OF AGRICULTURAL AND MECHANICAL ARTS WAS FOUNDED THROUGH THE DEVOTED INTEREST AND ZEAL OF HIS IMPERIAL MAJESTY HAILE SELASSIE I EMPEROR OF ETHIOPIA AND HIS MINISTERS, WITH THE ADVISEMENT AND COOPERATION OF THE GOVERNMENT OF THE UNITED STATES AND THE OKLAHOMA AGRICULTURAL AND MECHANICAL COLLEGE IN THE INTEREST AND FOR THE WELFARE OF THE PEOPLE OF ETHIOPIA IN THE YEAR 1952 A.D.

PRESENTED BY THE OKLAHOMA AGRICULTURAL AND MECHANICAL COLLEGE ON BEHALF OF THE CITIZENS OF OKLAHOMA AND OF THE UNITED STATES IN COMMEMORATION OF THE EVENT, AND IN TOKEN OF THE ESTEEM AND GOOD WILL IN WHICH THEY HOLD THE EMPEROR OF ETHIOPIA AND HIS PEOPLE THIS 18TH DAY OF JUNE, 1954.

Haile Selassie I subsequently had the plaque mounted in the cornerstone of the administration building at the new Alemaya campus. The Emperor gave citations and gold medals with green, gold, and red ribbons to Murray, Willham, and Darlow and made them officers of the Order of the Star of Ethiopia. In his remarks (again translated from Amharic by Endalkatchew), the Emperor praised A&M's "valued contributions" to his country and said:

"The successful program of technical assistance and economic cooperation to which the late President Bennett and many technicians from this great institution have made valued contributions is outstanding evidence of the mutual understanding which exists between our governments and peoples. I do hope that my visit to this great country will stimulate an even greater program of technical assistance and private capital investments."

After the dinner program, the Emperor joined Governor Murray and President Willham and their wives in a receiving line to greet some 1,600 guests invited to a reception in the Student Union Ballroom in honor of Selassie. After the first hour, those in attendance were asked to leave in order for the remainder of the guests to be able to get into the room. Among the guests Selassie met at the reception was William DeWitt of Coffeyville, a young army veteran of the Korean war who had been awarded bronze and silver stars and the Haile Selassie medal for bravery while assisting an Ethiopian battalion as a forward observer during heavy fighting.

Advance press releases had indicated that the Emperor would be in the line for only the first thirty minutes, but Selassie stood for an hour and forty minutes shaking the hands of almost everyone who came. The Emperor explained that he was pleased "the people came to see me, and they should be greeted." Selassie kept his right hand extended for each hand shake and accompanied it with a slight nod.

Upon completing his hand shaking ordeal, the Emperor took a seat on a huge chair in the banquet room--A&M's best approximation of a throne. Newspaper reporters present described Haile Selassie as "stern and dignified," "a solemn but friendly man" "with the face of an aesthete." The **Emperor**, again in a brief talk, expressed his thanks to A&M:

"I have made an exception to my usual practice on this trip in leaving my itinerary entirely and making this 2,000 mile trip in order to express to you my deep appreciation. This trip has given me the opportunity to visit a truly great agricultural and mechanical college. What I have seen here this afternoon has confirmed my conviction in the enormous possibilities which lie as yet still to be uncovered in Ethiopia."

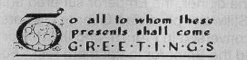

o all to whom these presents shall come
G·R·E·E·T·I·N·G·S

The Oklahoma Agricultural and Mechanical College of Stillwater, State of Oklahoma, United States of America, does by these presents formally express and certify its deep sense of respect and sincere admiration for:

HIS IMPERIAL MAJESTY
Haile Selassie I
Emperor of Ethiopia

and its sense of appreciation for his courageous and enlightened leadership of his people and his influential and beneficent influence and cooperation with men and nations of good will throughout the world, its sense of gratitude in the opportunity he has afforded this institution to assist him in some measure in bringing to fruition the humanitarian and progressive dream he holds for his great nation and its people, and its profound sense of honor that he has dignified this institution by his gracious personal visitation on this 18th day of June, 1954.

Attest:

P.E. Harrill
Secretary
Board of Regents

Earl Russell
Chairman
Board of Regents for the Oklahoma
Agricultural and Mechanical Colleges

Oliver S. Willham
President
Oklahoma Agricultural and Mechanical
College

When the reception came to an end at 10:00 p.m., Haile Selassie I held a private audience with members of the family of the late Henry G. Bennett--a measure of the high regard in which the Emperor held the former A&M president and Point Four director.[46]

During the night following the dinner, the Emperor suffered an upset stomach and had to have medical attention. Stillwater physician George Gathers was called at about 3:30 a.m. He and the Emperor conversed in French, and the doctor "administered opiates and sulfa drugs and advised the Emperor to get more rest." For his services, Gathers was paid with a solid gold medallion commemorating the Emperor's coronation.[47]

The dinner and reception were the biggest social events in A&M's history. The attire for those attending was strictly formal, "black ties and dark tuxedo coats for men (white jackets were acceptable for the dinner); formal dinner dresses either 'ballerina or full length' for the ladies. Local merchants reported that tuxedo rentals exceeded all demands previously set by fraternity parties, and clothing stores in Oklahoma City and Tulsa reported a brisk business in formal attire. An A&M student dormitory, Stout Hall, was opened to the public for the convenience of guests needing a place on campus to change into formal clothes.[49]

Oklahoma newspapers, especially the Stillwater Daily News-Press, the Tulsa Daily World, The Tulsa Tribune, and The Daily Oklahoman, played up the Emperor's visit with front page stories, photo coverage, and editorial greetings. The local media paid special attention to the young and photogenic Prince Sahle and Princess Sebla, who were described as "very charming, very poised."[50] A&M's student newspaper, The O'Collegian, using materials provided by the U.S. Department of State, published a series of three articles on Ethiopia and Haile Selassie I during the week of the visit.[51]

THE ROYAL PARTY DEPARTS

On Saturday morning, the royal party left Stillwater at 7:45 a.m. for their next destination, Mexico City. The President of Mexico, Ruiz Cortines, had phoned on Friday requesting that the Emperor arrive there at 1:00 p.m. This was a change of plans that resulted in the Ethiopians departing two hours earlier than planned. A scheduled auto procession down flag-draped Stillwater streets (from 9th to 5th down Main) was called off, and a tour of A&M farms became an abbreviated twenty-minute drive via College Avenue on the way to the airport. About 100 people including A&M's top officials were on hand for the Emperor's departure. Willham bid the royal party good-bye at the steps of the ramp leading up to the "Star of Bombay."[52]

[Taken from Theodore M. Vestal, Professor of Political Science, Oklahoma State University, "When the Emperor Came to Stillwater" http://fpokstate.edu/vestal/emperor]

H.I.M. Haile Selassie I in Stillwater, Oklahoma

Saturday, June 19: His Imperial Majesty arrives in Mexico City. The President of the Republic of Mexico, the Under-Secretary of Foreign Affairs, Minister of the Interior, Minister of National Defense, the President's Private Secretary, Chief of Protocol and Mexican Military Officials were at the airport to meet H.I.M. and gave H.I.M. full military honors.

Tuesday, June 22: His Imperial Majesty unveils a plaque on Plaza Ethiopia, named in His honor, together with the Mayor of the city. H.I.M. attends the Orthodox Church and later, at the Central Department, presented the Mayor with a medal. The Mexican Minister of Defense was also decorated by the Emperor, who visited Mexican industry and at Distriuidora Muebles Nacionales a banquet was offered in His honor. The Emperor visited Guadalupe shrine, where he donated a beautiful Ethiopian rug and fifteen thousand pesos. The Social Security Hospital was also visited by Emperor Haile Selassie.

THE ETHIOPIAN HERALD

1943

No. 1 - Vol. 12
Saturday, June 26, 1954

A WEEKLY NEWSPAPER
— PUBLISHED IN ADDIS ABABA

Subscription Rates (postage Included) In Ethiopia:
— 1 year: Eth.$ 6.24 — Six Months: Eth.$ 3.12 —
— Foreign (postage included) 1 year: Eth.$ 9.50 —

PRICE
Eth. 12 Cents

His Imperial Majesty Spends Few Days In Mexico Before Resuming Tour in The USA; Arrives in Great Port City of New Orleans

His Imperial Majesty's car passing through a Seattle street

B-U-L-L-E-T-I-N

NEW ORLEANS, Louisiana: June 24. — Emperor Haile Selassie arrived here today, after having left Mexico City with the President of Mexico and Government officials at the airport to see Him off. His departure was marked with a 21-gun salute.

At New Orleans airport to meet His Imperial Majesty were the Mayor of the city and an official civic welcoming committee. His arrival was marked with a 21-gun salute and military honors. In the afternoon the Emperor met leading citizens of New Orleans and was given the key to the city.

Later in the day, the Emperor was granted a citation at a ceremony at Dillard University and in the evening He was the honored guest at a reception and dinner at International House.

MEXICO City, June 19. — His Imperial Majesty and party arrived here today. The President of the Republic of Mexico, the Under-Secretary of Foreign Affairs, Minister of the Interior, Minister of National Defense, the President's Private Secretary, Chief of Protocol and Mexican Military Officials were at the airport to meet the Emperor, who was given full military honors.

MEXICO City, June 22. — Emperor Haile Selassie unveiled a plaque on Plaza Ethiopia, named in his honour, together with the Mayor of the city. He attended the Orthodox church and later, at the central department, presented the Mayor with a medal. The Mexican Minister of Defense was also decorated by the Emperor, who visited Mexican industry and at Distribuidora Muebles Nacionales a banquet was offered in His honour. The Emperor visited Guadalupe shrine, where he donated a beautiful Ethiopian rug and fifteen thousand pesos. The Social Security Hospital was also visited by Emperor Haile Selassie.

His Imperial Majesty is here seen arriving at a reception at the Rainier Club in Seattle

'Field Day' Held at Agricultural Technical School in Jimma

MANY DEMONSTRATIONS OF SCIENTIFIC FARMING ARE ILLUSTRATED

(By Our Own Correspondent)

JIMMA. — In conformity with His Imperial Majesty's plans for technical and scientific education, the Jimma Agricultural Technical School, a joint Ministry of Agriculture and Point Four institution, held its first "Field Day" exercises last Tuesday which was seen by a sizable number of farmers of

World's Food Supply May Be Raised by Applied Research

TI-BIOTIC DRUGS FORESEEN AS KILLING PLANT-DESTROYING PESTS

WASHINGTN. — Basic and applied research has been completed which will increase the world's food supply by assuring greater yields of nuts and vegetables. The research, conducted largely by scientists of the United States Department of Agriculture and of State universities, developed sprays of bacteria-killing antibiotic drugs which now control several serious plant diseases, two of which had been considered incurable.

U.S. Army Attaché In Swedish Instructors

Thursday, June 24:

When H.I.M. Haile Selassie I, arrived at Moisant Airport, a contradiction was immediately apparent. A dreadful roar came from a 21-gun salute from a Louisiana National Guard Unit. And, though his tan uniform was bedecked with row-on-row of ribbons, he stood as a gentle, peaceful being as the sun bore down. The Emperor stood at attention with right hand at salute through out the three-minute gun salute, acknowledging the honor as several hundred persons hung on the landing strip guardrails to get a better look at the Ruler.

At the airport to meet H.I.M. were the Mayor of the city and an official civic welcoming committee. His arrival was marked with a 21-gun salute and military honors. In the afternoon, the Emperor met leading citizens of New Orleans and was given the key to the city. Later in the day the Emperor was granted a citation at a ceremony at Dillard University and in the evening His Majesty was the honored guest at a reception and dinner at International House.

Said **H.I.M. Haile Selassie I**:

"The Principles that would maintain world peace in the 1930's and 1940's are the same that the world needs today," he said *"These are the strengthening of collective security and international morality and justice, It is by recognizing the eternal and universal validity of these principles that it will be possible to solve the problems provoking much of the unrest in the world today, and in particular, in those territories struggling for freedom or self-government."*

Emperor Haile Selassie I, a Coptic Christian, went on to tell of his favorite prayer in times of stress, "Come to me ye who are heavily burdened and I ...will give you peace." At His Imperial Majesty's press conference, the dreadful bearded Emperor said that the Supreme Court decision regarding segregation was *"in accord with the Constitution and one which would give the United States greater prestige in the world." "The Mutual Security treaty, which has been signed, is an important basis*, Emperor Haile Selassie I said, for co-operation between his country and the United States towards world peace. H.I.M. said that such co-operation would also bring to Ethiopia the prosperity it needs. "Would such co-operation be a one-way street?" He was asked. *"It is NOT a one-way proposition*," he replied, *"Ethiopia is prepared to give the United States the same degree of co-operation as the United States is prepared to give her."* The Emperor said he counted it a great honor to be made an honorary citizen of "this great city." *"I am mindful of the illustrious past and the progressive spirit of the present upon which the world-wide reputation of your city rests,"* he continued. H.I.M. also said he was also mindful *"of the significant role which the city of New Orleans played in the development of the middle and far west and of the role of constantly increasing importance which you are now playing in the development of world commerce."* The Emperor spoke in his native Amharic tongue and his words of thanks were translated into English by an interpreter.

The Mayor next personally introduced to the Emperor each member of the council. **Mayor Morrison** said in introducing H.I.M. to the guests at the International House *"If other Chiefs of State had his courage and foresight 20 years ago, many lives would have been saved and the world would not be in its current mess."* The Emperor and His party were guests at Dillard University for nearly two hours Thursday afternoon. Upon H.I.M. arrival, Emperor Haile Selassie I was shown about by Dr. Dent, University President and was then guest at a private reception in the President's residence. At the reception, many invited guests were introduced to the Emperor. Following the reception, Emperor Haile Selassie I was presented a citation by Dr. Dent in a public ceremony on campus. At this ceremony **H.I.M**. stated, *"It was a pleasure to meet those who are advancing the cause of the African people at home and abroad."* he said, *"The Principles of the Christian religion and indeed of good government everywhere require the observance of equality in human relation. By equality we mean the right for all people to make their respective contributions to the progress and development of the society in which they are called upon to live."* [Taken from Jahroots777, H.I.M. Visits New Orleans, http://www.geocities.com/jahroots777/himvisitno.htm]

Friday, June 25:

His Imperial Majesty arrives at Fort Benning, Georgia.

Saturday, June 26:

During the morning, the Emperor was officially welcomed to Fort Benning by a twenty-one gun salute fired by a battery of the forty-first field artillery battalion. Honor Guard troops reviewed by His Majesty were from the second battalion of the thirtieth infantry regiment. Music was provided by a composite eighty-piece army band. Following the Guard of Honor **Emperor Haile Selassie** I attended briefings covering the infantry school, witnessed an airborne demonstration which he later referred to as being *"especially impressive"* and observed an infantry-tank demonstration. At an official luncheon **His Imperial Majesty** pointed out that, *"it is not difficult to understand why the United States even from its infancy has always emerged victorious from every war. The new arms and techniques which you are developing here and of which you have given today so magnificent a demonstration are now being made available to my country under an agreement completed last year. This association is the source of great pride and satisfaction not only to myself but to my people. Moreover our comradeship with you in arms under conditions of actual combat in Korea has already served for us as another Fort Benning. Thanks to the mutual security agreement it will be possible for the Ethiopian soldier to conserve and advance yet and to continue with you a comradeship in arms dedicated to the defense of collective security."* Emperor Haile Selassie I then honored three Fort Benning officials by bestowing upon them decorations from his country. Major-General Joseph H. Harper, infantry center and infantry school commandant and Brigadier-General Carl F. Fritzsche, assistant commandant, were awarded the Grand Cordon of the Distinguished Order of the Star of Ethiopia as *"a further token of the happy relations which exist between our two governments and our respective armed forces."* Colonel John Hightower, deputy-assistant commandant of the infantry school and project officer for the Emperor's visit to Fort Benning was officially presented the Commander of the Distinguished Star of Ethiopia which has been previously authorized. The **Emperor** also presented an ivory trophy to the infantry school *"as a symbol of the contribution of peace through collective security within the charter of the United Nations Organization."* His Imperial Majesty expressed great confidence in the Ethiopian officers (two) sent to the infantry school for training. His Imperial Majesty then departed at 3:00 p.m. in a chartered TWA airplane, "The Star of Bombay" for New York City.

THE ETHIOPIAN HERALD

No. 2 - Vol. 12
Saturday, July 3, 1954

A WEEKLY NEWSPAPER
PUBLISHED IN ADDIS ABABA

Subscription Rates (postage included): In Ethiopia:
— 1 year: Eth.$ 6.24 — Six Months: Eth.$ 3.12
— Foreign (postage included) 1 year: Eth.$ 9.50 —

PRICE
Eth. 12 Cents

His Imperial Majesty is Back in New York After Extensive Tour in United States And Side Trips to Canada and Mexican Republic

His Imperial Majesty is here seen in a car with the President of Mexico

Annual School Sports Day Is Held by Asella School

GOVERNOR-GENERAL OF ARUSSI PROVINCE ATTENDS THE DISPLAY

Our Special Correspondent

ASELLA. — Annual Sports Day of the Ras Dargay School, Asella, took place last Saturday afternoon on the play field of the school. His Excellency Dejazmatch Mengesha Seyoum, Governor-General of the Province of Arussi, Her Highness Princess Aida Desta and His Beatitude Abuna Lukas attended.

Churchill, Eisenhower End Washington Talks

UNITED EFFORTS PROMISED

WASHINGTON. — Sir Winston Churchill and President Eisenhower, ending their talks here, announced that they would continue united efforts for world peace and disarmament. Their long week-end of informal, candid conversation concluded with a declaration of basic common principles underlying Anglo-American policies in which they reaffirmed the Atlantic charter.

The two leaders said they would continue "to hold out the hand of friendship" to any and all nations which by word and deed showed themselves desirous of a just and fair peace.

They would not agree to treaties which would subordinate formerly sovereign states "now in bondage" and they would seek unity of nations, divided against their will, through free elections under United Nations.

Churchill and Eisenhower discussed their declaration with their foreign secretaries Eden and Dulles at the White House.

'Banana Republic' Said Misnomer for Guatemala

NEW YORK. — Commercial circles here point out that one of the misconceptions current in some quarters abroad is that Guatemala is a so-called "Banana Republic" that the U.S.

This picture shows a reception given by His Imperial Majesty at the Waldorf-Astoria Hotel in New York

U.S. Army Training Camp Is Emperor's Final Tour Stop

GREAT INTEREST SHOWN IN TRAINING OF AMERICAN INFANTRY

FORT BENNING, Georgia. — Emperor Haile Selassie of Ethiopia left Fort Benning Saturday afternoon apparently greatly impressed with the United States infantrymen, and with the deep conviction that his visit to this country has strengthened the bonds of friendship between the two nations.

Before taking off in a chartered

Examinations Are Now Being Held in Schools

THOUSANDS TAKING TESTS

By Our Own Reporter

The month of June here each year is the time of final examinations. In all educational institutions in the country these tests are held now, immediately before school closing, to determine what the students have absorbed during the school year.

In the primary schools, when last year, objective mental ability tests were introduced of a non-credit character in order to begin an intelligence quotient series adaptable to Ethiopia. This year's tests in Amharic, English expression and comprehension, mathematics, science and social studies were based on the Otis series of tests and are still in the experimental stage.

Nation-Wide

The nation-wide General Examinations for elementary schools for the eighth grade were held at all schools in the provinces and in Addis Ababa.

Ethiopian Herald No. 1 Vol. 12 Saturday, June 26, 1954 courtesy of IES

Wednesday, June 30:

His Imperial Majesty visited the headquarters of the American Bible Society and accepted the organization's offer to sponsor the printing of fifty thousand copies of the "Sermon on the Mount" in Amharic. The translation from the Gospel according to Saint Matthew will be taken from a revised manuscript of the Amharic Bible, which is now being completed in Ethiopia under the Emperor's direction. Doctor Eric M. North, General Secretary of the American Bible Society, which translates and publishes bible texts for fifty Christian denominations, presented the Emperor with a copy of the King James Bible and a copy of the Revised Standard Version.

Saturday, July 3:

His Imperial Majesty Visits Bronx Zoo, Bible Society

EMPEROR PRESENTED EXQUISITE KING JAMES VERSION OF BIBLE

NEW YORK. — Emperor Haile Selassie made a surprise visit to the Bronx Zoo last Saturday. The trip was his own idea, and the Emperor seemed to enjoy his visit. Pictures in the New York newspapers showed the Emperor smiling and relaxed at the zoo, which is located in the Bronx borough, one of the five boroughs of New York City.

A member of the zoo staff said His Imperial Majesty laughed heartily when one of the zoo keepers staged a wrestling match with Oka, the lady gorilla. Later the Emperor entered a pen housing three jaguar cubs and a baby tiger named Fer. He smiled broadly as he petted Fer, held by the keeper of the Zoo's animal nursery.

Sees Tussle

The Emperor and his party also enjoyed viewing the fish in the Acquarium. A twenty-foot python in the reptile cage, baboons, and penguins partaking of a late afternoon snack were watched.

When the Emperor returned to the Waldorf-Astoria Hotel, his secretary said he had enjoyed everything but the weather which had been too warm and unlike that of Addis Ababa.

NEW YORK. — Emperor Haile Selassie last Wednesday visited the headquarters of the American Bible Society and accepted the organization's offer to sponsor the printing of fifty thousand copies of the "Sermon on the Mount" in Amharic.

The translation from the Gospel according to Saint Matthew will be taken from a revised manuscript of the Amharic Bible, which is now being completed in Ethiopia under the Emperor's direction.

Gift

Doctor Eric M. North, General Secretary of the American Bible Society, which translates and publishes bible texts for fifty Christian denominations, presented the Em-

Emperor Haile Selassie I makes surprise visit to the Bronx Zoo. A member of the zoo staff said His Imperial Majesty laughed heartily when one of the zoo keepers staged a wrestling match with Oka, the lady gorilla. Later the Emperor entered a pen housing three jaguar cubs and a baby tiger named Fer. He smiled broadly as he petted Fer, held by the keeper of the Zoo's animal nursery. The Emperor and his party also enjoyed viewing the fish in the Aquarium. A twenty-foot python in the reptile cage, baboons, and penguins partaking of a late afternoon snack were watched. When the Emperor returned to the Waldorf-Astoria Hotel, his secretary said he had enjoyed everything but the weather that had been too warm and unlike that of Addis Ababa.

Above: New York: H.I.M. examines a baseball given him by New York Yankee Baseball team manager Casey Stengel before the start of a game at Yankee Stadium. Though it was the first big league baseball game the Emperor had ever seen, he watched with interest and seemed to enjoy the American sport.

Below: New York: H.I.M. obliges a cameraman by posing with a baseball fielder's glove during his visit to Yankee Stadium to watch a game of baseball. With the Emperor and his aides, are members of the Mayor's reception committee.

Ethiopian Herald No. 3 Vol. 12 Saturday, July 10, 1954 courtesy of IES

Monday, July 12:

His Imperial Majesty Haile Selassie I departs from the United States Monday night on a chartered plane for Nice, France. From there His Imperial Majesty will visit Marshal Tito in Yugoslavia, then Greece, and return to Addis Ababa on August 3, 1954. **His Imperial Majesty** thanked Americans for the *"friendliness and hospitality"* they showed H.I.M. during His visit.

Ethiopian Herald No. 4 Vol. 12 Saturday, July 17, 1954 courtesy of IES

His Imperial Majesty Left United States
Thanked Americans for Their Hospitality

NEW, YORK JULY 12. — Emperor Haile Selassie left the United States by plane tonight. The Emperor, boarded with his party of 16, a chartered airliner for Nice, France.

From there he will go to Belgrade to visit Marshal Tito of Yugoslavia. The stay in Yugoslavia, which is at Marshal Tito's invitation, is expected to last from four to six days.

His Imperial Majesty thanked Americans for the "friendliness and hospitality" they showed him during his visit and said he was sorry to leave the United States.

Selassie Begins U.S. Visit May 25

ADDIS ABABA, Ethiopia (NNPA)— Although not yet officially decided, Emperor Haile Selassie of Ethiopia will most likely visit England towards the end of the year, after touring the United States and Canada.

A visit to Great Britain would be his first since he left there, after spending his exile in London, to return to his country after it was freed from the Italians by the British.

The Emperor left here May 19 and is due to arrive in New York on May 25.

Political significance is becoming increasingly attached to the Emperor's visit to the United States because of the recent upswing of interest in Asian and African affairs.

It is regarded as a well-timed, renewed sign of alliance with the Western Powers and as a fresh gesture of antipathy towards communism.

It also shows to other African, Middle Eastern and Asian governments that Ethiopia is taking a realistic view of world affairs.

In connection with the projected visit to Great Britain, the Emperor is interested in strengthening trade ties of the two countries. The Ethiopian government is seeking to encourage investment in this country. The Emperor said he would particularly welcome investment from Britain and the British Commonwealth.

The Ethiopian government is very much concerned with economic development. That question overshadows most political issues.

British officials and business men in Addis Ababa would also like to promote British competition in this healthy market. They feel that British business is missing excellent opportunities while other countries, particularly the United States, Holland and Germany, are showing much more activity.

Bishop W. M. Roberts, 78, Drops Dead

Bishop William M. Roberts, of 6214 S. Michigan ave., nationally-known spiritual leader who founded the Church of God in Christ in Illinois, died suddenly of a heart attack last Monday on his 78th birthday.

He was stricken as he entered his car in front of his home about 10:45 a.m., on his way to the market at 63rd st., and S. Parkway. He was pronounced dead on arrival at St. George hospital.

A state funeral will be held Friday noon at Roberts' Temple Church of God in Christ, 4021 S. State st., where he pastored. A final service will be conducted Sunday noon at the church. Burial will be in Burr Oak cemetery.

Officiating at the rites will be Bishop C. E. Bennett of Indiana and Bishop O. T. Jones of Pennsylvania. Other dignitaries attending the funeral will be Senior Bishop C. H. Mason; Dr. Arenia C. Mallory, president of Saints Industrial and Literary school at Lexington, Miss.; James Scott, assistant Over-

See BISHOP — Page 2 Col. 2

Chicago Defender, May 1954

Haile Selassie Arrives, Asks U. S. Investments

NEW YORK, May 25 (UP)—
Haile Selassie I, Emperor of Ethiopia, arrived today for a tour of
America and a state visit with
President Eisenhower.

In a shipboard interview as the
liner United States passed the
Statue of Liberty, the thin, 62-
year-old "Lion of Judah" said that

"by far the most important" thing
said he had a massage every day
America could do to invest private
capital in Ethiopian railroads, mineral resources and agriculture.

The Emperor declined to comment on reports he is prepared to
grant America military bases in
Ethiopia. However, it was learned
from a diplomatic source that it
is expected a Washington announcement soon will disclose
America will be given a long-
term lease on a military base
there.

Haile Selassie said he did not
plan to discuss uranium supplies
during his Washington visit, which
will begin tomorrow when he flies
to the capital in the President's
private plane for three days of
state ceremonies.

It was announced "10 days ago
that high-grade uranium ore had
been discovered in Ethiopia. However, today the Emperor, in answer to press questions, said he
"hoped there is uranium in the
country—that is something to
study in the future."

Arriving with a large royal and
servant entourage and accompanied by his youngest son and a
granddaughter, the five-foot four-
inch "Elect of God" wore his Field
Marshal's tan uniform, with 51
medals on his left chest.

On the five-day Atlantic crossing
the Emperor wore business suits,
replacing the robe of pure woven
gold which he wears when he sits
on the throne in Addis Ababa as
ruler of the oldest Christian realm
on earth and direct royal descendant of King Solomon and the Queen
of Sheba.

He mingled with passengers,
but seldom spoke. Ship officials

and attended movie matinees
daily. Each morning at 7 he

Woman Bookie Gets $100 Fine on U.S. Charge

Mary Clemens, 37, of Broadway,
Ipswich, the first woman bookie
to be indicted under the Wagering
Tax Law of 1951, was today given
a $100 fine, a six months' suspended sentence and probation for
two years by Federal Judge Francis J. W. Ford.

The defendant, a hairdresser,
entered a plea of guilty to charges
of failing to register as a bookie
and failure to purchase the $50
occupational tax stamp.

Back Bay Man Hurt

FALL RIVER, May 25—A Boston taxi driver escaped serious
injury early today, but a passenger was seriously injured when
the vehicle went out of control and
bounded over 100 yards. Boston
knocking down several obstructions before overturning and
catching fire.
Edward Franco, 30, of 234 Roxbury st.

Short and Sweet

FREMONT, Neb. May 25 (AP)—
When the time came to let the
candidates talk at the Republican
State pre-primary election convention here they were warned to stay
within a five-minute time limit by
State Chairman W. W. Spear.
Atty.-Gen. Clarence S. Beck,
seeking reelection, did it easily.
His address: "Thank you Bill
... Greetings to you all and God bless
you."

Wheat was cultivated early in
the Stone Age.

BOSTON BOUND—Emperor Haile Selassie I of Ethiopia, waves on arrival in New York aboard liner United
States. The 61-year-old bearded ruler is official guest of
President Eisenhower. With him is his granddaughter,
Princess Sybel Desta, 23-year-old Oxford University student. The famed Emperor will be in Boston June 3.

pulled an overcoat over his pajamas and strolled the upper deck.
He ate American food on the
crossing, letting his suite steward
choose the menu.
Haile Selassie stopped over in
United States and at 8:40 a.m.
E.D.T. after standing at salute
while the New York Fire Department Band played the national anthems of the United States and
Ethiopia. As the liner docked the
band had erected the Emperor
with "O, What a Beautiful Morning."
The Emperor said that on his

ELMIRA, N.Y. May 25 (AP)—
There were 200 delegates on hand
last night when firemen doused
a small blaze in the kitchen of the
Mark Twain Hotel.
The delegates were here from delegates
at the 25th annual conference of
the Eastern Association of Fire
Chiefs.

Boston Daily Globe May 25, 1954

Foreign News

Haile Selassie in U. S., Seeks Private Capital

Emperor Silent On Reports Of Deal for Bases

NEW YORK, May 25 (UP). Haile Selassie I, emperor of Ethiopia, arrived today for a tour of America and a state visit with President Eisenhower.

In a shipboard interview as the liner United States passed the Statue of Liberty, the thin, 62-year-old "Lion of Judah" said that "by far the most important" thing America could do for his African nation would be to invest private capital in Ethiopian railroads, mineral resources and agriculture.

The emperor declined to comment on reports he is prepared to grant America military bases in Ethopia. However, it was learned from a diplomatic source that it is expected a Washington announcement soon will disclose America has a long-term lease on a military base there.

Haile Selassie said he did not plan to discuss uranium supplies during his Washington visit, which will begin tomorrow when he flies to the capital in the President's private plane for three days of state ceremonies.

It was announced 10 days ago that high-grade uranium ore had been discovered in Ethiopia. However, today the emperor, in answer to press questions, said he "hoped there is uranium in the country—that is something to study in the future."

Arriving with a large royal and servant entourage and accompanied by his youngest son and a granddaughter, the five-foot four-inch "Elect of God." wore his field marshal's tan uniform, with 51 medal ribbons on his left chest.

Haile Selassie, whose family name is Ras Tafari Makonnen, bears numerous titles among which are "King of Abyssinia, king of kings of Ethiopia, Lion of Judah, the Elect of God, King of Zion, branch of the tree of Solomon and Implement of the Holy Trinity."

HAILE SELASSIE
. . . won't talk uranium

Indo Victory Up to U. S., French Say

War Must Soon Be Broadened, Military Men Think

BY JIM G. LUCAS
Scripps-Howard Staff Writer.

HANOI, May 25.—American intervention?

Both the French here and the Viet Namese are convinced that the Indochina War will never be settled at Geneva. They think the solution can come only on the battlefield, and it can be resolved favorably only if America pitches in.

From that starting point, their views diverge—for instance, as to timing.

"If you Americans don't come within a month, we are lost." said a Viet Namese businessman.

Said a French officer: "If we can hold six months, we may not need you. After all, the native army is coming along. With conscription in effect and junior officers being turned out at a good rate, six months more would make the Viet Namese Army, a real factor."

Yet, most military men agree with the French commander in chief, Gen. Henri Navarre, that if the war is to be won it must be "internationalized." Junior officers and enlisted men—those who are being killed and wounded every day—have grown tired of fighting a war with too little, too late.

Even so, they discuss the possibility of our intervention with misgivings.

"This is what worries me," said one young French officer. "We know that if you come in, so will the Red Chinese. But America is 12,000 miles away and China is only 90 miles distant. Sure; you'll win in the long run, but we wonder if we'll be around to help you celebrate."

Some Viet Namese, for example, not only want us to intervene, they sincerely hope we will take over from the French thereafter.

Communist Rise in Guatemala Is Building Toward Climax.

BY CHARLES LUCEY
Scripps-Howard Staff Writer

GUATEMALA CITY, May 25. The trappings of trouble lie heavy on this sleepy little land that is tense today in a rise of Communism that is pushing the old two-bit Central American revolution into discard.

There seems an utter incredibility in the positions of the Guatemalan and U. S. governments in a situation which responsible sources here believe, despite some calming words from the Guatemalans yesterday, is building steadily toward a climax.

This difference emerged in an interview in which Foreign Minister Guillermo Toriello belittled the idea of a Red ascendancy here in the heart of the Western Hemisphere. He said his country never could become another Czechoslovakia, to be taken into the Moscow camp.

But observers outside the government say that unless the present trend is checked in this new pro-Communist government it will be Red-controlled in 18 months. These observers describe today's situation as "dangerous and insist that time is running on the side of the Reds.

Red China Called Unfit for UN Seat

CHICAGO, May 25 (UP). Henry Cabot Lodge Jr., chief United States representative at the United Nations, today charged "the Chinese Communist regime is wholly unfit" for UN membership. He promised the U. S. would "steadfastly resist all maneuvers" by the Communist regime to "bribe its way" into the UN.

Lodge charged that the Peiping regime is guilty of "international promotion of drug addiction" and that it "has conducted an international extortion racket."

Lodge, speaking before the Inland Daily Press Association, also accused the Communists of "direct" aggression in Korea,

"concealed" aggression in Indochina, and "internal" aggression against the Chinese people.

Yesterday, after a 90-minute meeting with U. S. Ambassador John C. Peurifoy, Toriello said the groundwork had been laid for talks to end a tenseness that has been mounting since 2000 tons of arms from behind the Iron Curtain were dumped into Puerto Barrios on the Atlantic coast.

Toriello described the talk as a friendly one which gave hope that problems between the two countries can be resolved. The U. S. embassy said nothing. But there was no sign of any enthusiasm.

Basically, the meeting went to the question of Guatemalan expropriation of nearly a quarter million acres of lands of the United Fruit Co. Toriello formally rejected the fruit company's claim of some $16,000,000 for land which Guatemala proposes to pay less than $600,000.

It is understood that Guatemala may be ready soon to make some counter proposal to the company's claim. But Toriello, in an interview following the meeting, belted the fruit company with everything he had for its past practices here.

He charged that the fruit company is financing the attempts of Guatemalan exiles in nearby Central American countries to lead a rebellion against the present Guatemalan regime of President Jacobo Arbenz.

Toriello provided the customary answer about Reds in government by saying they held not a single cabinet post. But he acknowledged some of them are in the government agency administering the sweeping agrarian reform movement to which the United Fruit land grab contributed.

Toriello fails utterly to understand the nature of Communism and the tactics of Communists, they say, when he professes to believe that Guatemalan Red leaders trained in

Red control.

As for the arms shipments, the facet they see most alarming is the size. Two thousand tons, they say, is an immense supply for a country with an army of only 6000 or 7000 men —enough to arm not only this country but all Central America.

"I'm your Coal Dea and I have a will help us

YOU GAIN 3 WAYS BY ORDERING N

1 You'll enjoy knowing that your coal and off your mind . . .

2 You won't run the risk of even one ho cold or damp house should cold come before you're prepared for it . .

3 Coal in the bin is like money in the ban

When you order, specify Fuel Sati This is the superior Bituminous Coal along the Norfolk and Western. It ha the choice of practical-mixed home t

---

A MOST AMAZING TIMEPIECE

The Very Watch for Graduation and Father's Day

Cincinnati Post May 25, 1954

Selassie Wants $100,000,000

WASHINGTON — Two days after Emperor Haile Selassie arrived in the United States on his state sponsored tour, it was learned that the ruler of over 19,000,000 persons in Ethiopia was laying groundwork for a loan of $100,000,000 to help develop natural resources in his country.

Details of the loan must still be worked out in conferences of State and Treasury Department officials with Ethiopian officials.

Reliable souces said that the Conquering Lion of Judah desired the money for the development of rich uranium deposits in Ethiopia, for establishment of a school of engineering to give university training to likely Ethiopian students and for the establishment of a modern Ethiopian hospital in his capital, Addis Ababa.

Selassie is said to favor a loan rather than a grant because a loan would leave his country free to develop its own ore and other resources and retain independence in deposing of the production.

It was also learned here through government comment that the Emperor would have little resistance to his requests, partly for his friendly attitude toward the Western powers in the face of offers to Ethiopia by Communist powers.

Another probable reason Selassie will get the loan without resistance is because of the tradition of Ethiopia's complete independence and because it exercises an influence among Africans far out of proportion to its size.

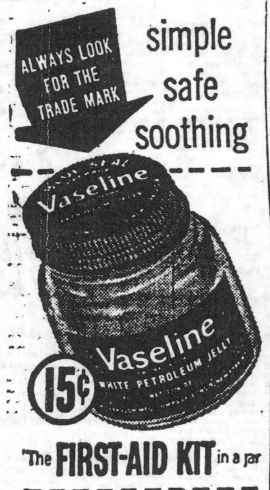

Chicago Defender, June, 1954

Washington Post May 26, 1954

Haile Selassie Arrives Today; U. S. Workers Get Off Early

Emperor Haile Selassie I of Ethiopia is scheduled to arrive at National Airport at 4 p. m. today and receive an official welcome to Washington as part of his 50-day tour of this country, Canada and Mexico.

The five-foot, 61-year-old Selassie and his party of 18 will be greeted with full military honors at the airport and escorted along a flag-bedecked route to the District Building, where he will be presented keys to the city in ceremonies at 4:30 p. m.

Federal employes will be dismissed at 3:30 p. m. to witness his arrival, and District employes at 3:45. Seventeen military and school bands will provide a musical welcome and 5000 Ethopian flags will be distributed.

The party will cross Memorial Bridge, take 23d st. to Constitution ave., thence to 12th st., to Pennsylvania ave., to the District Building for the ceremony, and to the White House at 5 p. m., where the Emperor will be received by President and Mrs. Eisenhower.

Included in the itinerary of the Emperor's three-day visit here are the placing of wreaths at the Tomb of Washington at Mount Vernon and the Tomb of the Unknown Soldier in Arlington on Thursday. On Friday, Emperor Selassie will attend a special service at Washington Cathedral at 9:30 a. m. and will address a joint meeting of Congress at 12:30 p. m.

The party will leave Saturday morning for Princeton, N. J.

Washington Post May 26, 1954

35,186.

Entered as Second-Class Matter.
Post Office, New York, N. Y.

May 26, 1954

NEW YORK, WEDNESDAY

UTE
RGE
RTS

kings
ences
re

USED'

unters
runks
s

of the
nd 17,

E
s.
25—A
ed tele-
h back
arthy's
raining
David
orm.
ublican
charts
by the
evision

three
ed to-

ted in-
re two
y the
Schine
N. J.,
of his
n the
e pri-

Ethiopia's Emperor Lands Here Amid Noisy Welcome

INDO
FOR
ON

Military
Native
Cam

Text o
Inc

B
Spe
WASH
Indochir
slipping
and is n
ed Stat
choice o
interven

Secre
at a new
of mora
Nations
by the
in Indo

The
china
more de
censore
Hanoi a
make th

¶A
Delta a
about
munist
being,
atively
forts o
the delt
have to
perimet
Haiphor

¶The
among
Commu

The New York Times

Haile Selassie, Emperor of Ethiopia, Conquering Lion of the Tribe of Judah and Elect of God, puts finger to ear to soften din as he arrives on liner United States. At left is his granddaughter, Princess Sybel Desta, and at right, Richard C. Patterson Jr. of reception committee.

By PETER KIHSS

Haile Selassie of Ethiopia, Emperor of one of the world's most ancient territories, arrived here yesterday. He voiced the hope that—with American private investment—his country might swiftly develop modern opportunities. A dignified figure in a red-trimmed khaki field marshal's uniform with nine full rows of medals, he looked far younger than his 61 years. His thick black hair and beard had no touch of gray. His regal bearing made him seem taller than his 5 feet 4 inches. As the liner United States warped into Pier 86, West Forty-sixth Street, he brushed aside Ethiopian and State Department advisers who wished him to avoid answering

Continued on Page 8, Column 3

New York Times, May 26, 1954

Associated Press Wirephoto

PRESIDENT WELCOMES HAILE SELASSIE: President Eisenhower greets Emperor on north portico of the White House as he arrives for a state visit. Mrs. Eisenhower is beside her husband. The Emperor's granddaughter, Princess Sybel Desta, is at center, and Emperor's son, Prince Sahle, stands beside his father. Party will tour the U. S., Canada and Mexico.

New York Times, May 27, 1954

Text of Haile Selassie's Address to U. S. Congress

Special to The New York Times.

WASHINGTON, May 28—Following is a translation of the text of the address by Emperor Haile Selassie I, before a joint session today of the Senate and House of Representatives (the Emperor spoke partly in English and partly in Amharic):

I count it a privilege to address what is one of the greatest parliaments in the world today, where the forces that make great one of the most powerful of nations have been and are being brought to bear and where issues of world-wide importance have been decided.

The extent of that power and influence and the rapidity with which you have reached such a summit of importance for the rest of the world are unparalleled in world history and beggar all conceivable comparisons.

Two hundred years ago today, as I am speaking, Gen. George Washington won the Battle of Fort Necessity, a victory which was but a step in the gradual forging together of the United States.

What a phenomenal progress has been made in that interval of two hundred years, an interval which—you may pardon me as representative of one of the most ancient nations in the world—is surely but a surprisingly short passage of time.

So great are your power and wealth that the budget of a single American city often equals that of an entire nation.

As in the case of other countries, you gave us Lend-Lease assistance during the war and, at present, both Mutual Security and Technical Assistance. Yet, so vast are your power and resources that even after deducting all expenses of the Federal Government, you have met the costs of this assistance in one-quarter of an hour—fifteen minutes—of your annual production.

Of what interest is it to you then, you may well ask, that I, the head of what must be for you a small and remote country, should appear before you in the midst of your deliberations?

I do not take it upon myself to point out why Ethiopia is important to the United States—that you can best judge for yourselves—but, rather, to explain to you with brevity, the circumstances which make Ethiopia a significant factor in world politics.

Since so much of world politics is, today, influenced by the decisions which you, members of Congress, reach here in these halls, it is, perhaps, not unimportant that I set out these considerations for you.

A moment ago, I remarked that, for you, Ethiopia must appear to be a small and remote country. Of course, both of these terms are purely relative.

Associated Press Wirephoto

CONGRESS HEARS ETHIOPIAN EMPEROR: Haile Selassie as he appeared yesterday before a joint session. In the rear are Vice President Richard M. Nixon, left, and Joseph W. Martin Jr., Speaker of the House. The Emperor said that no state, "large or small," could refuse the call of another for assistance in fighting against aggression.

marked us, like you, in giving more than lip service to these ideals.

It is your deep comprehension of our ideals and struggles in which it has been my privilege to lead, at times not without heartbreak, my beloved people, and our common comradeship in arms that have laid a very sure and lasting basis for friendship between a great and a small country.

Dollar-Based Currency

Last year, we concluded with you a new treaty of friendship, commerce and navigation designed to assure to American business enterprise expanded opportunities in Ethiopia. Our dollar-based currency is also there to assure the ready return to the United States of the profits of their investments.

We have entrusted to American enterprise the development of our civil aviation, which has surpassed all expectation. To American enterprise we have confided the exploitation of our oil resources as well as of our gold deposits.

Although my country is 8,000 miles removed from the Eastern seaboard of the United States, United States exports to Ethiopia have, notwithstanding this heavy handicap, pushed forward to the forefront in Ethiopia.

Conversely, the United States stands in first-rank of countries to whom we export. Ethiopia, which has, from the province of Kaffa, given the world the name and product of coffee, produces on her high plateau one of the finest Mokka coffees in the world. The coffee which you drink attains its unique and pleasant American flavor in part, at least, through the added mixture of Ethiopian coffee. American shoes are made, in part at least, from Ethiopian goatskins, which are principally exported to the United States.

On the other hand, you have given us valuable support, not only in Lend-Lease assistance during the war, and today through Mutual Security and Technical Assistance agreements, but you have also powerfully aided us in obtaining rectification of long-standing injustices.

If, today, the brothers of Ethiopia stand finally united under the crown and if Ethiopia has regained her shoreline of the Red Sea, it has been due, in no small measure to the contribution of the United States of America.

I am happy to take this occasion to express to you, the Congress, which has approved this assistance, the sincere and lasting appreciation of my people.

Collaboration With West

This collaboration with the West, and with the United

the last world war, Ethiopia has become a new frontier of widely expanding opportunities, notwithstanding the tremendous setback which we suffered in the unprovoked invasion of our country nineteen years ago and the long years of unaided struggle against an infinitely stronger enemy.

The last seven years have seen the quadrupling of our foreign trade, currency and foreign exchange holdings. Holdings of American dollars have increased ten times over. The Ethiopian dollar has become the only

broader sense is Ethiopia's geographical position of significance. Through her location on the shores of the Red Sea and in the horn of East Africa, Ethiopia has profound historical ties with the rest of the Middle East as well as with Africa.

In this respect she stands in a completely unique position. Her culture and social structure were founded in the mingling of her original culture and civilization with the Hamitic and Semitic migrations into Africa from the Arabian peninsula, and, in

New York Times, May 29, 1954

Plans before the school board call for a start on ending segregation next fall, with complete desegregation one year thereafter. The board then recessed until next week without a formal vote on the timing.

The plans were laid down before the board by Hobart M. Corning, superintendent of Washington schools. They are designed to put into effect as rapidly as possible the Supreme Court decision of May 17, holding racial segrega-

opening school term next September and for "complete desegregation of all schools" by September, 1955.

The five points are, in brief:
1. All assignments and ratings in the school system shall be based on merit, not race or color.
2. No pupil shall be favored or discriminated against because of race or color.
3. Children in no event shall be permitted to attend schools outside their boundaries in which they live for reasons of race or color.
4. No records of pupils or personnel shall make any preference to race or color.
5. All schools shall be used to maximum efficiency without regard to race or color.

The board has nine members—six white members and three Negro members. And although the plan was adopted by a 6-to-2 vote, after Negro members pushed for a quick decision, points 3 and 4 raised a flurry of questions.

Whites Earn 20 Times Native Pay In Kenya

UNITED NATIONS, N. Y. (ANP) A recent report issued by the United Nations points out the wage discrepancy between non-white and white workers in strife-torn Kenya. The average earnings of Africans is $73, that of Asians and other non-whites, $774, while that of the whites is $1,848.

The figures are for yearly income.

Integration On Display For Selassie At Capital

By JAMES L. HICKS

WASHINGTON, D. C.—(NNPA) —Colored Washingtonians were much in evidence both in official and non official capacities here

Wednesday as the nation's capital greeted Emperor Haile Selassie, the Emperor of Ethiopia.

Although the reports persist that Ethiopians do not consider

themselves as kindred to colored Americans, the government lost no opportunity to present colored Americans in a favorable light during the Emperor's stay here.

It was obvious that the State Department realized that his visit on the heels of the Supreme Court decision offered a good opportunity to counter Communist racial propaganda which has plagued this nation in world forums.

Three colored policemen were in the official escort of 26 policemen who rode ahead of the pro-Emperor west through Washington to the White House.

At the airport the armed services saw to it that there were many colored servicemen in evidence. The Third Infantry Regiment which provided the official honor guard had a large number of its colored soldiers from the second battalion "right up front."

Prior to last year the regiment had refused to accept colored soldiers.

Among those on hand from the Third Regiment Wednesday were Pvts. Edwin Ferguson, Bluefield, W. Va., Elbert Grace, New Bedford Mass.; Cornelius Clark, Dunn, Hartford, Conn.; Pfc. Thomas Mc-Queen, Boston; Pfc. Bertram Carter, Buffalo, N. Y.; Pfc. Le Drue Ware, Oklahoma City, Okla.; Cpl. N. J; Pfc. Edward Jones, Dayton, Ohio; S-Sgt. Hulit Bullock, High Point, N. C.

The Air Forces had a public relations officer on duty to handle the press at the airport and all along the route where military men snapped to salute there were large numbers of colored servicemen.

At the reviewing stand set up in front of the District Building where the Emperor received the key to the city there was an additional number of colored citizens in the official welcoming group.

16 Persons Accompany Selassie On U. S. Tour

WASHINGTON — When Emperor Haile Selassie arrived here last week and was greeted by President Eisenhower, he had with him a 16 member entourage that was expected to grow by leaps and bounds as the tour progressed.

Members of his royal party included a prince and a princess and even a minister of war. Their names and royal titles are as follows:

His Imperial Highness Prince Sahle Selassie Haile Selassie, third son of the Emperor; Her Highness Princess Sebla Desta, granddaughter of the Emperor; Gen. Abeye Abbebe, Minister of War; Tsahafi Yohannes, Minister of Justice and Minister of the Pen; Akilou Wold, Minister of Foreign Affairs, and Tafarra Wold, the Emperor's private secretary.

Others are Col. Makoanen Denneke, Aide-de-Camp to the Emperor; Endalkatchew Makoanen, Chief of Protocol, Ministry of Foreign Affairs; John Spencer, senior advisor, Minister of Foreign Affairs and Bitwodded Dr. Zervos, personal physician to the Emperor.

Joining the entourage in New York were Yilma Deressa, Ambassador of Ethiopia; John F. Simmons, chief of Protocol; Joseph Simonson, American ambassador to Ethiopia, Major Gen. Arthur G. Trudeau, American aide to the Emperor; Vincent Wilber, press officer, Department of State and John F. McDermott, security officer, Department of State.

Army Private Publishes Novel

Chicago Defender, June, 1954

Four

2 'Solar Boats' of Egyptian King Found Intact After 5000 Years

CAIRO, May 26 (AP)—Two 5000-year-old "solar boats" that belonged to Egypt's King Cheops were dug up today in perfect condition from sands beside the Great Pyramid of Giza.

The find was announced tonight by Kamal el Mallakh, government director of excavation works in the Pyramids district.

He said he made the discovery while clearing a car track around the Great Pyramid.

He said diggers going under the foundation yesterday came through a long corridor "which we thought would lead to Cheops' southern tomb. This morning we found the corridor did not lead to the tomb. But shortly after we commenced new digging we rejoiced because we believe these two intact solar boats are even more important than finding the tomb."

The boats, which figured in the sun-worshipping beliefs of the ancient Egyptians, are 120 feet long and 18 feet wide. El Mallakh said they were packed with wooden furniture and numerous statues of King Cheops made of a "peculiar aromatic wood."

The importance of the discovery lies in the fact the boats are the only relics belonging to the Cheops era—apart from the pyramid—known to exist today. All other relics have been destroyed or stolen.

The excavations director said he believed that when his work is completed it might form the most important archeological discovery in many years.

Moslem Count

India's population includes 43,-000,000 Moslems.

WATCH REPAIRING

5 DAY SERVICE
1 YEAR GUARANTEE

NO CHARGE FOR MINOR REPAIRS
MAIN SPRINGS REPLACED $2.50

SALE! WATCH BRACELETS
R. H. WHITE'S — STREET FLOOR

Emperor Selassie Calls For Collective Security

BY JAMES L. HICKS

WAHINGTON, D. C.—Emjeror Haile Selassie stood before a joint session of Congress Friday and called on the world to apply the principle of collective security "whatever the cost."

The Conquering Lion of the Tribe of Judah made his plea in a dramatic 35 minute address before this nation's top government officials during which time he spoke for 32 minutes in his native Amharic tongue, the official language of his government

With Vice President Nixon presiding and five Justices of the Supreme Court and other high cabinet officials present, the Ethiopian monarch, whose country was overrun by the Italians in 1936, said collective security can succeed only if it is backed by a determination "to apply it universally both in time and space but also whatever the cost."

Received by Warren

Emperor Selassie addressed the special session a half hour after his official visit here had taken him to the Supreme Court Building where he was received by Chief Justice Warren and four other Associate Justices who donned their black robes to welcome him in the Chief Justice's chambers.

He entered the joint session which was held on the House side of the Capital, promptly at 12:30 and received a thundering standing ovation from the members of both houses of Congress and the capacity audience which packed every seat in the galleries.

Prior to his entrance Vice President Nixon arrived and took over the speaker's gavel. The Emperor was then escorted to the speaker's podium by five Senators and five Representatives selected by the Senate and House.

Scholarly Presentation

The Emperor's speech was a clever scholarly presentation of the role being carved out for Ethiopia in the world today. He pointed out how eighteen years ago he had appealed to the League of Nations for aid when his country had been overrun by Italy and he told how when that aid failed to come "I personally assumed before history the responsibility of placing the fate of my people on the issue of collective security..."

He pointed out that his actions marked the first time in world history that the collective security issue "was posed in all its clarity."

"My searchings of conscience convinced me" he said, "of the rightness of my course, and if, after untold suffering and indeed, unaided resistance at the time of aggression, we now see the final vindication of that principle in our joint action in Korea. I can only be thankful that God gave me strength to persist in our faith until the moment of its recent glorious vindication."

After having thus rightfully pictured his nation as the spearhead of collective security the Emperor then went on to point to the strategic importance of his nation as a bulwark of aggression in Africa.

The Emperor only mentioned the word "race" once in his 35 minute talk. That came when he said in speaking of his country:

"On the other hand, three thousand years of history make of Ethiopia a profoundly African state in all that that term implies. In the United Nations she has been to the forefront in the defense of Africa's racial, economic and social interests."

In the huge crowd which thronged the galleries were many colored Washingtonians, and others came from Baltimore to hear the speech.

Among those glimpsed were Elmer Lindsay, Lois Lippman, White House secretarial aide, and Mrs. Carl Murphy of Baltimore.

Congressman Adam Clayton Powell was in his seat on the floor and had with him some members of the Emperor's official party. Princess Selba Desta and Madame Deressa, wife of the Ethiopian Ambassador sat in a choice seat in the gallery and warmly applauded the Emperor. The Emperor's son, Prince Sahle Selassie was also present.

Toasts Exchanged by Eisenhewer, Selassie

WASHINGTON, D. C.—The following toasts were exchanged by President Eisenhower and Emperor Haile Selassie Wednesday night when the President and Mrs. Eisenhower gave a dinner in honor of the Emperor at the White House:

The President to the Emperor:

"Your Majesty, ladies and gentlemen:

"During the past century and a half there have been entertained within these walls many individuals of distinction—some of out own country some visiting us from abroad.

"I think it is safe to say that never has any company here gathered been honored by the presence in their guest of honor of an individual more noted for his fierce defense of freedom and for his courage in defending the independence of his people than your guest of honor this evening.

"I read once that no individual can really be known to have greatness until he has been tested in adversity. By this test, our guest of honor has established new standards in the world. In five years of adversity, with his country over-run but never conquered, he never lost for one single second, his dignity, he never lost his faith in himself, in his people and in his God.

"I deem it a very privilege, ladies and gentlemen, to ask you to rise and with me to drink a toast to his Imperial Majesty, the Emperor of Ethiopia."

The toast was then drunk and the Emperor responded in these words:

"I thank you Mr. President, for the kind sentiment which you have expressed on this occasion, because I take them, not as addressed to me, but to my beloved people.

"I have accepted your kind invitation, Mr. President, to come to the United States and visit your nation, because it has offered me the occasion to express the

(Continued on Page THREE-C)

Selassie Receives Key to The Capital

WASHINGTON, D. C.—(NNPA) — With President Eisenhower greeting him as a "defender of freedom and a supporter of progress" Emperor Haile Selassie of Ethiopia was given the key to the nation's capital Wednesday as official Washington roared him a welcome.

Accepting the welcome with the dignity of the king that he is, Emperor Selassie told the President and the American people that for years "it has been one of my fondest hopes to be able in person to convey to the President and the people of the United States the expression of the profound admiration which I and my people have for your great nation."

The White House and the State Department left no stone unturned to give the Ethiopian ruler the full plush velvet treatment and

Selassie Educates Ike During Washington Tour

WASHINGTON, D. C. (NNPA) —President Eisenhower told his press conference Wednesday that he received from Haile Selassie I, Emperor of Ethiopia, a very elementary education which he should have had before.

Mr. Eisenhower made his statement when he was asked if he cared to comment upon the Emperor's visit.

He would say this: Not only did he have a very interesting visit with the Emperor, but a very enlightening one, Mr. Eisenhower replied.

Among other things, he said, the Emperor brought along an industrial map of Ethiopia, showing the industries of various sections, and also brought him a few products of his country.

Mr. Eisenhower said he was ashamed to say that the Emperor had given him some very elementary education he should have had before.

He described the Emperor as a charming individual and said the people with him were interesting and knew their business.

He is certain that in Ethiopia, Mr. Eisenhower declared, there is a deep underlying appreciation of America's efforts and affection for the people.

Chicago Defender, June, 1954

The New York Times

The New York Times

GIFTS FOR THE MAYOR: Emperor Haile Selassie presents two mounted elephant tusks, a warrior shield and two spears to Mr. Wagner during official reception for the monarch at City Hall. Standing at the left is the Emperor's interpreter.

New York Times, June 2, 1954

VISITING EMPEROR HAILED IN PARADE

A Million Cheer Selassie in File Up Lower Broadway to City Hall Ceremony

OVATIONS CROWD THE DAY

Monarch Is Honored Guest at Waldorf-Astoria Luncheon and Reception at U. N.

By MURRAY SCHUMACH

People by the hundreds of thousand, words by the tens of thousand and paraders by the thousand were marshaled yesterday by the city to honor Haile Selassie I, Emperor of Ethiopia.

With deed, word and gift, the city accorded the ruler of 19,000,-000 persons a welcome he later called the most wonderful he had ever received.

From the confetti blizzard of a ticker-tape parade to the last echo of after-dinner praise, the Conquering Lion of Judah went through a day of ovations that included a reception at City Hall; an official luncheon at the Waldorf-Astoria Hotel and a reception at the United Nations.

In explanation of the city's tribute, Mayor Wagner told the 62-year-old monarch that here, "the home of the United Nations, we recognize deeply and with full comprehension the struggle which you have undergone and the progress which you have achieved, and we take great pride in the place you have earned for yourself and your country in the history of the world."

The Emperor replied that since the city had obviously opened its heart to him he no longer needed the key he had received. He hoped this hospitality was an indication that cultural and commercial ties between the United States and Ethiopia would be strengthened

Congratulations GRADUATES

Three Pages of Pictures

of State and City

Graduates—Section D

CLEVELAND Call and Post

Ohio's Fastest
Growing Weekly

Entered as 2nd Class Matter at Post Office, Cleveland, Ohio, under Act of March 8, 1879

VOL. 49—NO. 19

CLEVELAND, OHIO, SATURDAY, JUNE 5, 1954

Welcome for Ethiopian Emperor

BULLETS NUMBERS

Seawright, Boone Homes Hit; Police Quiz Rival Bosses

By MARTY RICHARDSON

A full scale resumption of the bloody policy war which took nine lives in the 1930's and which has been smouldering again for the past several months, appeared to have broken out Sunday morning when shotgun blasts tore holes in the homes of William Seawright and Daniel Boone.

The shooting-up of the two homes was the first violence noted here in the numbers field in many months, although there had been rumors for a long time that something in due

'Get Tough' is

Cleveland Call and Post, June 5, 1954

HONORS FOR VISITING ROYALTY: Washington — According to persons who have served in one capacity or another in connection with visits of heads of state to Washington, Emperor Haile Selassie I of Ethiopia, was given one of the warmest receptions ever accorded any head of state in the past eighteen years during his three-day visit here.

Top photo shows the Emperor receiving the key of the city from a district commissioner when he arrived in Washington last week. Watching the proceedings closely is his second son who seldom removes his gaze from his distinguished father. At the extreme right is the Emperor's granddaughter Princess Shella Desta, whose beauty and charm have created a mild sensation among diplomatic corps (Below) Dr. Mordecai Johnson of Howard University is seen conferring an honorary degree upon the visitor at a special ceremony at the university. (CALL-POST Photos by Oscar Williams)

* * * * *

Selassie Cites Kinship Between Darker Peoples

BY JAMES L. HICKS

WASHINGTON, D. C. — Emperor Haile Selassie identified himself and the people of Africa with the colored people of America Friday, and said the United States would never have reached its present world stature were it not, in part, for the work of Africans whose descendants are the colored Americans of today.

The Emperor's direct association of his people with the colored people of America came as he accepted an honorary degree of doctor of laws from Howard university and it exploded the oft repeated, but never confirmed rumor, that the Ethiopians do not wish to be identified with colored Americans.

10,000 On Hand

An estimated 10,000 persons were on hand to witness the special ceremonies at which the Emperor was honored.

The Howard university special convocation exercises was the first predominantly colored audience before which the Emperor has appeared since being in this country and he selected the occasion to make his first public utterance about the colored people of this nation.

Accepting the award as a "tribute to my people" and a tribute to the "contributions of the peoples of Africa everywhere" the Emperor said:

"It is certain that the United States of America would not have reached today its present world stature, were it not, in part, for the enormous labours of Africans whose great descendants are here represented on this occasion.

"You are continuing that tradition in expanding the new frontiers of thought and science here in these halls of Howard university through the intelligence and efforts of peoples of African origin.

The Emperor's originally prepared (Continued on Page THREE-A)

Seawright, B Homes Hit; P Quiz Rival Bo

By MARTY RICHARDS

A full-scale resumption of the blood took nine lives in the 1930's and which again for the past several months, appe out Sunday morning when shotgun blas homes of William Seawright and Daniel

The sho homes wa ed here h many mon been rumo "something loose"...

The Sur were follo matic dev

Police h ery known clearing-ho tor, dragg ters for de

Police C nounced a under whic ders to ar bers figur to be jail out again found abou them spen their lives money on quarters sa

Tension known spe pecially al that short ings there an East S target for selected, a

A split largest sin had been p smaller ho a large pa itself.

Sit Underlyin a critical ling racket late Bennie ago caused made whe put heavy number.

These big lowering of (Continued

'Get Tough' is New Order for Numbers Game

The newest police order to "get tough" on operators of Cleveland's badly-disorganized numbers and clearing house games, had already resulted in a series of arrests and crippling raids before it had been in effect 24 hours.

Within a few hours after Police Chief Frank Story's order that all known and suspected numbers operators were to be arrested on sight and brought in for questioning, Alex "Shondor" Birns was arrested as he rode with a friend in an automobile on the Lorain-Carnegie Bridge. The friend was released, but Birns was hauled in for questioning about the recent outbreak of violence in the numbers racket.

In another swift action, police struck at the headquarters of Willie "Burkeye" Jackson, who allegedly was operating in a basement at 1144 E. 125 St. Jackson fled the raiding party, leaving behind him most of his numbers office equipment including records that indicated that his operation had grossed about $3000 last Friday.

Other familiar figures in the once-lucrative numbers and police (Continued on Page THREE-A)

Hit-Skipper Kill In Record Holid

The long Memorial Day weekend extending through Monday, took a national death toll of 484, far over the National Safety Council estimate of 340. In Ohio alone, the

three day fatalities fr accidents, numerous I

Linda Jo St., was in in St. Luk fell from t daughter of Jones, she opened the just as her off from a

---

Prison Looms for Witnesses in Trial of 'Prophet' Tonelli; Two Charge 'Doublecross'

Cleveland Call and Post, June 5, 1954

Ike Educated By Selassie During Visit

WASHINGTON, D. C. (NNPA)—President Eisenhower told his press conference Wednesday that he received from Haile Selassie I, Emperor of Ethiopia, a very elementary education which he should have had before.

Mr. Eisenhower made his statement when he was asked if he cared to comment upon the Emperor's visit.

He would say this: Not only did he have a very interesting visit with the Emperor, but a very enlightening one, Mr. Eisenhower replied.

Among other things, he said, the Emperor brought along an industrial map of Ethiopia, showing the industries of various sections, and also brought him a few products of his country.

He described the Emperor as a charming individual and said the people with him were interesting and knew their business.

He is certain that in Ethiopia, Mr. Eisenhower declared, there is a deep underlying appreciation of America's efforts and affection for the people.

Greater Wealth

Dublin — Eire, called the poorhouse of Europe in 1840, today has one of the highest per capita wealths in its history.

Early Park

Little Rock—Hot Springs reservation in Arkansas is one of the nation's oldest national parks. It was established in 1832.

THE EMPEROR DISAGREES

State Department Given Kingly Rap On Official Wrist

By JAMES L. HICKS

NEW YORK, N. Y.—Emperor Haile Selassie gave the U. S. State Department and the City of New York a mild but kingly rap on the wrists Wednesday when he decorated a Harlem man whom the U. S. officials had ejected from a luncheon held in the Emperor's honor.

The rap came when the Emperor awarded the Star of Ethiopia decoration to James C. Lawson, head of the Universal Nationalist African Movement in Harlem.

Lawson, long a controversial figure in Harlem, had incurred the wrath of the City by organizing a committee which he called the "Official Committee" for the Visit of Haile Selassie to New York. The committee was set up before the Emperor arrived here May 25.

When members of the committee began to visit Harlem merchants and ask them to buy ribbon and bunting to display when the Emperor arrived, the Harlem Uptown Chamber of Commerce called the Mayor's committee and asked who was the official committee.

Only One Committee

The Mayor's committee then held a press conference which was

(Continued on Page SIX-C)

Keep Ethiopia Up-to-Date On Selassie Visit

WASHINGTON, D. C. (NNPA)—The press and radio services of the U. S. Information Agency, a Government agency, is giving the people of Ethiopia special daily on-the-spot accounts of the visit of Emperor Haile Selassie to the United States.

Extensive arrangements were made by the agency for detailed coverage of this historic event. A press, radio and photo team is assigned to provide complete reporting of the Emperor's tour and special arrangements were made for immediate transmission over-

Cleveland Call and Post, June 1954

THE EMPEROR OF ETHIOPIA

The Book which we should constantly read tell us that "princes shall come out of Ethiopia" and next Thursday, June 3, that prophecy will be fulfilled in Boston and vicinity when Emperor Haile Selassie of Ethiopia will be guest of the Commonwealth of Massachusetts and the City of Boston. This monarch heads one of the oldest, reigning houses in the world, tracing his descent from the Queen of Sheba, of whom King Solomon was enamoured. For centuries his ancestors governed their territories in unbroken succession until the Italian Fascist invasion of 1935 forced Haile Selassie into temporary exile at Bath, England. Those of us who are old enough will remember how the Emperor eloquently asserted at the League of Nations that his country was "the last citadel of collective security." He declared that the West perish if it did not come to the aid of Ethiopia with sanction against Mussolini's aggression. We all know how nearly fulfilled was

over the split in the old League of Nations when the question of Italian aggression in his little country became international news back in 1935. The subsequent vacillation of the Big Powers and the concomitant passions in neighboring territories of Africa.

mind as such, for them to deduce from exclusive interviews that Ethiopians, and especially the Emperor himself, are totally unaware of the current developments in neighboring territories of Africa.

his prophecy by World War II when all anti-fascist mankind walked in the valley of the shadow.

Today this wise African ruler is an historic symbol. His chief adversary perished ignobly in a five-and-ten store lynching. He returned from exile to rebuild his country along modern lines as an enlightened despot like Peter the Great of Russia or Frederick the Great of Prussia. Today there are few hereditary monarchs anywhere, and the long-range trend of history is to eliminate all of them. However, the emperor will find that, although we Bostonians, like the rest of our fellow Americans, are democrats and republicans in the marrow of our bones, we delight in honoring monarchs and titled aristocrats.

Boston Chronicle, May 29, 1954

Boston Chronicle

See Page Eight For Week's Pictures

VOL. XXXIX, NO. 23   BOSTON, MASS., SATURDAY, JUNE 5, 1954   PRICE FIVE CENTS

Haile Selassie Visits Hub

Rita Hayworth's Ex-Brother-in-Law Joins NAACP Here

By Edna L. Harrison

Prince Sadruddin Khan, who is now attending Harvard University, purchased two NAACP life memberships on Tuesday, June 1. Mrs. Katherine Coleman, secretary of the Robert Gould Shaw House, was directly responsible for this thoughtful gesture, since it was Mrs. Coleman who had the foresight to approach the prince on the possibility of his taking the memberships.

The prince, who is the son of His Highness the Aga Khan, ruler of the Ishmaili sect of the Mohammedans (that is the potentate who every year receives his weight in precious metals gold and platinum, from his followers all over the world) and also younger brother of Aly Khan, ex-husband of movie star Rita Hayworth, was Eartha Kitt's constant companion when she appeared here recently at the Latin Quarter.

Col. Larkland Hewitt, president of the Boston Branch of the NAACP, and Kivie Kaplan, leather merchant who has done so much for our local NAACP, and who is also a life member himself, were overjoyed when Mrs. Coleman presented them with the thousand dollar check in the office of the NAACP, 784 Tremont Street.

Your reporter cannot help but feel a little responsible for this happy event since she was instrumental in introducing Mrs. Coleman to Eartha Kitt and subsequently to Prince "Sadri" Khan.

Columbia L. H. D. To Lester Granger

NEW YORK—Lester B. Granger, executive director of the National Urban League since 1941 and one of the nation's leading social workers, is one of thirty-three men and women who received honorary degrees from Columbia University at its commencement exercises on June 1. The honorary degree of Doctor of Humane Letters was conferred upon him.

He has received many awards and honors, among them the C. I. O. 1944 Award for Outstanding Work in Race Relations, and honorary degrees from his alma mater, Dartmouth College, from which he was graduated in 1918. He has also received honorary degrees from Oberlin, Morris Brown, Wilberforce, and Virginia Union.

Howard Univ. Graduates 600

WASHINGTON, D. C.—The Honorable Louis C. Cramton, former Congressman from the State of Michigan, delivered the 86th annual Commencement address at Howard University Friday, June 4.

More than 600 students in the University's 10 schools and colleges were awrded degrees bby Dr. Mordecia W. Johnson, president of the University, during the exercises. Three honorary degrees were conferred. They went to Chester Bowles of Essex, Conn., former ambassador to India; Thurgood Marshall of New York City, special legal counsel for the National Association for the Advancement of Colored People; and Roy W. Bornn of St. Thomas, V. I., commissioner of social welfare for the Virgin Islands.

Graduates from Massachusetts are as follows: Henry D. Bell, Cambridge, M. D.; Manuel Nunes, West Wareham, M. D.; John J. Goldsberry, 3 Palmer St., Worcester, B. S.; Joseph P. Johnson, Howland St., Boston, B. S.; Janet F. Murphy, 161 Townsend St., Boston, B. S. and Consuelo M. Sousa, 111 Bay Village, New Bedford, B. S.

Bunche to Address B. U. Graduates

Commencement at Boston University will be held Sunday, June 6, at 4 o'clock, in Boston University Field with President Harold C. Case presiding. Dr. Ralph Bunche, director of the Trusteeship Division of the United Nations, will address the approximately 2300 members of the graduating class. Honoray degrees will be presented to a group of distinguished persons. This will be the first time that Commencement has taken place on the University's campus. Previously the exercises have been held in the Boston Garden which, in case of rain, will be used this year.

DR. RALPH J. BUNCHE

The traditional Baccalaureate Services, to be addressed by President Case, will also take place on Sunday, in the morning at 10:30, also in Boston University Field. President Case has chosen as his theme of his parting message to the graduates, "Design for Qualified Leadership." In case of rain, this will take place in Boston Garden.

A full academic procession of faculty, administrative officers, and students will open both programs.

Annual Prince Hall Memorial Rites

Sunday afternoon, the Most Worshipful Prince Hall Grand Lodge, F. & A. M., of Massachusetts, held its annual Memorial Day services at Copps Hill Burying Ground, Hull St. in traditional tribute to the founder of Negro Masonry in America, M. W. Prince Hall.

Rev. Samuel L. Laviscount, the senior grand chaplain, gave the invocation. R. W. Cleo Wooten, K. T., 33rd degree, related a brief history of the Grand Lodge. Past Grand Master, Dr. William D. Washington of Lynn, K. T. 33rd degree made the presentation of the wreath. The eulogist for the occasion was R. W. Wilfred S. Bailey, Deputy Grand Master. M. W. Dr. James R. Lesueur, K. T. 33rd degree, Grand Master, gave an address.

Oscar Dunham, R. W. Frederick J. Timberlake, K. T., R. W. George A. Berry, K. T. and R. W. James A. Reyaleon, added to the

Conquering Lion Of Judah Thrills Many Thousands

By William Harrison

Although circumstances permitted him to visit Boston and vicinity for only six hours, His Imperial Majesty Emperor Haile Selassie I, Conquering Lion of the Tribe of Judah, King of Kings, Elect of God, came, saw, and conquered last Thursday. From the moment that the emperor and his entourage of twenty persons, including his beautiful granddaughter, Her Imperial Highness the Princess Sybel Desta and his third son, His Imperial Highness Prince Sahle Selassie Haile Selassie, arrived at Logan Airport, East Boston, at 10 o'clock that morning, until their departure in a Royal Canadian Air Force plane at 3:30, a royal welcome was given to this "leader whose very name arouses our respect and admiration," according to Mayor John B. Hynes of Boston.

State and City Unite To Honor Potentate

At a joint session of the state legislature in the House Chambers, to tumultous applause from legislators and cheers from the gallery, Emperor Haile Selassie spoke briefly in Amharic, his native language, and his speech was translated by his interpreter, Endelkatchew Makonnen, chief of protocol. He declared: "It is my fervent hope that you legislators will serve the people properly and that Almighty God will give you guidance." Later, on the initiative of Reps. Herbert L. Jackson of Malden and William A. "Billy" Glynn of Roxbury, the legislature unanimously passed resolutions lauding the emperor and an embossed parchment of the text was later presented by Rep. Jackson to him at the Sheraton Plaza luncheon tendered him by Governor Christian H. Herter and

Mayor Hynes.

The emperor signed the City Hall guest book and chatted briefly with City Council President Joseph C. White, Councillor Francis X. Ahearn, and Victor C. Bynoe, Commissioner of Veterans Services, highest ranking Negro official in the city government. Hundreds lined the streets near City Hall and along the route taken by the motorcade to Cambridge, where the imperial party stopped to be received by President Nathan M. Pusey at Harvard University in Massachusetts Hall and to walk to Houghton Library to view the first book printed in Africa in 1516, Ethiopic manuscripts and other treasures relating to Ethiopia.

Mayor Emcees Luncheon

Master of ceremonies at the Sheraton Plaza luncheon was Mayor Hynes, who introduced for bows members of the consular corps from various countries among whom were Consul General Francois Charles-Roux of France, Jean-Louis Delisle of

Continued on Page 8

Deaconesses To Aid Elderly Ladies

The Deaconess Baptist Union, of which Deaconess Kelly is president, will give its first benefit Sunday, June 13, at 4 p. m., at 558 Mass. Ave., to aid elderly women and to assist in lessening juvenile delinquency. Guest speaker will be Mrs. Harold McKenney, a lady noted for her help to men and women of all races and walks of life. An excellent program is promised.

Chairmen of the event are Deaconess Obeline H. Lamb and Mary Smith. Subscription is 50 cents.

Tomb of King, 4700 Years Old, Found Under Unfinished Pyramid

CAIRO, June 3 (AP)—Discovery of the oldest untouched tomb of one of Egypt's ancient Pharaohs containing a sarcophagus of reddish alabaster was disclosed tonight by an Egyptian archaeologist.

The discovery was made at Sakkara, about 20 miles south of the Giza Pyramids, where other antiquarians are in the process of uncovering the solar boats which Pharaoh Cheops, of the fourth dynasty, is presumed to have built to carry him on his journey through the Heavens after death.

The newly discovered tomb is believed to be that of Sankhet,

of the third dynasty, who ruled Egypt about 2750 B. C.—4700 years ago.

His golden coffin is expected to be found inside the sarcophagus in the rock funeral chamber into which Zakaria Goneim burrowed last Monday.

TOMB
Page Eight

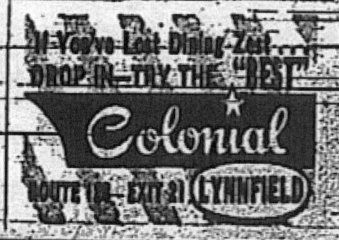

Boston Daily Globe June 4, 1954

"ALWAYS PLAYED FOR KEEPS"
The Great Lionel Conacher
By VICTOR O. JONES

Boston to Welcome Ruler of Ethiopia

By JOAN McPARTLIN

RULER OF A LAND WHERE MORE THAN 50 LANGUAGES are spoken, Emperor Haile Selassie dispatched Ethiopian soldiers to help another country—Korea. Ethiopia is a member of the United Nations; a battalion of Ethiopians, under this flag, fought in Korea.

THE RAS OF RASSES, Lord King of Kings of Ethiopia, Conquering Lion of the Tribe of Judah, the Elect of God and the Light of the World. Who is he? Haile Selassie, Emperor of Ethiopia.

Crosby Looks at Despair
Wanted: More Sunshine
By JOHN CROSBY

Odd Items From Everywhere

WITH THE AID OF BRITISH OFFICERS AND SOLDIERS, the Emperor (here with English officer), returned to Africa in 1940. With British arms and leaders, Ethiopian soldiers moved back into their homeland and recaptured it.

SELASSIE'S KINGDOM. Ethiopia shown (black) on map of Africa.

"KING OF KINGS"

Haile Selassie met President Roosevelt on a United States warship near Cairo. The President was returning from the "Big Three" Conference in Yalta.

DENNIS THE MENACE By Hank Ketcham

"What's after you THIS time!"

RESTORED RELATIONS WITH ITALY were marked when the Emperor received Giovanni Brusasca, Italian Under-Secretary of Foreign Affairs, in the throne room at his palace in 1951.

ETHIOPIA'S EMPEROR has had a busy schedule since arriving in the United States. His visit at the White House was the high spot.

(Globe Photo by William Ennis)

EMPEROR VISITS HARVARD—Haile Selassie and President Nathan Pusey in Harvard Yard.

Jailing Methods on Wrong Track, Penologist Says

FRAMINGHAM, June 3—Longer jail sentences and other techniques of repression, without a program of rehabilitation, "may set penology back 100 years," a New York correctional authority told the annual meeting of the "Friends of Framingham" here tonight.

Judge Anna Kross, New York city commissioner of correction, termed the mere jailing of offenders "a false measure of security."

Judge Kross addressed members of the Friends of Framingham, "Friendly Visitors" and "Friends of Prisoners of Massachusetts, Inc.," meeting at the Women's Reformatory here.

Among the speakers were state Correction Commissioner Reuben L. Lurie, Judge Jennie Loitman Barron of Boston Municipal Court and Reformatory Supt. Dr. Miriam Van Waters.

Mrs. Edgard J. Driscoll, Boston, was elected president of the "Friends" during the annual business meeting. Other officers elected were Lawrence E. Corcoran, Rev. William J. Wiltenburg and Dr. Neal B. DeNood, vice presidents; Mrs. Cynthia Thomas, secretary, and Allan H. MacDonald, treasurer.

EMPEROR
Continued from the First Page

Into his flying visit he packed a speech to the House of Representatives, a visit to see African manuscripts at Harvard's Houghton Library and a short address to a room full of city and State officials at the Sheraton.

"Too often abroad one is impressed with the material strength and importance of the United States," said the Emperor, speaking in his native tongue of Amharic. (An interpreter stood by his side constantly, though the Emperor speaks French and English fluently.)

"Less often have we the occasion to probe the tremendous depth and wealth of America's cultural heritage and achievements. . . .

"We have been tremendously impressed with the wealth of learning amassed around the City of Boston in institutions of unparalleled influence in cultural and scientific fields."

Harvard Greeting Warmest

He was presented two silver bowls, a scroll, drawn up and read by Representative Herbert L. Jackson of Malden, and a slim volume called "Introduction to Harvard," by Pres. Nathan M. Pusey.

By the time the Emperor left Houghton Library and entered his car, students had formed a human aisle through which the motorcade passed. The Emperor, smiling with pleasure, stepped into the car as students burst into applause. He sat down, then stood up as the clapping continued, removed his officer's cap (he was dressed in a field marshal's uniform) and bowed with great dignity to the cheering students.

At the luncheon at the Sheraton, consuls of many countries, Gov. Herter and Mayor Hynes, and several city and state officials gathered to honor the royal party.

Dr. E. Joseph Evans of Newton Centre was among the guests called to the head table to meet the Emperor personally. Dr. Evans recently visited Haile Selassie in Ethiopia to discuss the establishment of a Christian school and college.

The Emperor, who had breakfast in Washington and lunch in Boston, dined last night in Ottawa. He left Boston at 4 p.m. on a Royal Canadian Air Force transport.

HOUSING
Continued from the First Page

Senator Maybank, Dem., of South Carolina tried to knock out all public housing authority, but the Senate rejected this on a voice vote.

Lower Down Payments

The Senate version would lower down payments and lengthen repayment periods for homes bought with government-insured mortgages.

It continues the farm housing program and contains safeguards against "windfall" profits and other scandals which have plagued the Federal Housing Administration in recent months.

The legislation does these other things:

1. Tightens up on the home-repair loan program and leaves the maximum loan at $2500 and the terms at three years, Mr. Eisenhower asked a liberalized program.

2. Continues the Federal National Mortgage Association as the government's secondary market for privately-held mortgages. The President has asked that this operation be gradually turned over to private control.

3. Inaugurates a smog-clearance program with a $5,000,000 research fund to the government.

4. Boosts the direct-loan program to veterans to $200,000,000 a year.

B. U. Scholarship to Honor Speare Revealed at Fete

Funds totaling $22,500 have been raised to establish an E. Ray Speare scholarship at Boston University, it was announced last night as more than 400 friends and colleagues met at Hayden Hall to honor Speare, who retires in October after 51 years as B. U. trustee and 20 years as treasurer.

The scholarship will be awarded annually, State Senator Edward C. Stone, B. U. board chairman, announced. Stone also presented Speare with a gold wrist watch from the trustees and an album of letters from friends and associates.

Chancellor Daniel L. Marsh praised Speare, 81-year-old financier, businessman and sportsman, as a "versatile and pioneering man" and a "high-grade Christian gentleman."

Luck Is Cat-ching

Mrs. Ida Archibald, 73, of 40

SCIENTISTS
Continued from the First Page

The latter, an appointee of former President Truman, will leave at the end of the month and be replaced by an Eisenhower appointee.

The Federation of American Scientists urged not only that the A. E. C. review the case again but also that the entire machinery of government security come under review.

"We believe the majority findings to be unfair to Oppenheimer," the federation said. "But more than that, we believe them to illustrate the dangers and the bitter fruits of a security system which is now motivated more by the risks of politics than the risks of disclosure of information."

The majority report of the personnel Security Board on Dr. Oppenheimer, it said, "bears the imprint of fair-minded men struggling unsuccessfully against the pressure of a security system extended beyond reasonable bounds."

"The fault lies at least in part," the federation said, "in criteria so loosely and generally drawn that they can even admit to serious consideration, in estimating security status, such fantastic assertions as lack of enthusiasm for official policy. The threat lies in the use of security machinery to dispense with technical consultants whose views may no longer be acceptable to the Administration in office. The danger lies in the discouragement of independent-minded men, including many scientists, from lending their talents to government."

(Boston Globe-N. Y. Herald Tribune.)

School Buses

School buses are in such growing use they account today for about 70 percent of the total bus output in the United States.

Boston Daily Globe June 4, 1954

Boston Chronicle

See Page Eight For Week's Pictures

Haile Selassie Here June 3

Last Segregated U.S. Army Unit Gone

The last segregated Unit in the United States Army is now being dissolved. The Secretary of the Army so informed Rep. Adam Clayton Powell, Jr., 16th Congressional District, N. Y., and invited the N. Y. Congressman to inspect this new integrated unit, the Mess Detachment of the 1,002nd Regiment of the United States Military Academy at West Point.

Last Saturday, May 22, Representative Powell inspected the unit, and was the luncheon guest of the Commandant of the Military Academy.

On Parole Board

JULIAN D. STEELE, moderator of West Newbury, Mass., and recently elected moderator of the Congregational Christian Churches of Massachusetts was appointed last Thursday to the State Parole Board by Governor Christian A. Herter. One of the most notable citizens in New England, Mr. Steele is an honor graduate of Boston Latin School (1925) and Harvard College (1929). He was formerly headworker of the Robert Gould Shaw House, executive director of the Armstrong-Hemenway Foundation, and president of the Boston NAACP branch.

Pusey Deplores D.C. Club Jimcrow

Washington—In reply to a question designed to embarrass him at the conclusion of his speech on "Freedom, Loyalty, and the American University" at the luncheon meeting of the National Press Club here Tuesday, May 25, President Nathan Marsh Pusey of Harvard University came off with flying colors. He was asked how he felt about the decision of the Harvard Club of the District Club of the District of Columbia to vote Thurs-
(Continued on page 5)

King of Kings

HAILE SELASSIE

IONICS in Annual Cabaret Dance at Dorchester Plaza

Have you ever had the feeling that something taking place had happened exactly the same way before?

That's the way you are going to feel at the Sixth Annual Cabaret Dance presented by the Ionics at Dorchester Plaza, 5 Tonawanda St., Friday evening, June 4, 1954, from 8 o'clock.

This gala affair is brought to you and yours by a group of matured men. It took them more than three months to prepare this program of music and dance for your satisfaction, and the major added attraction is the floor show interspersed with the modern calypso.

The music of Buster Daniels' Orchestra is the sweetest this side of Massachusetts.

The affair is informal. It is given every year at the same place where music lovers meet and enjoy the fun. Sandwiches and beverages will be available.

Don't miss it! Call the Chronicle office, ask for Ernie Headley about your ticket.

Memorial Service For Mrs. Raven

Sunday, June 13, at 7:30 p.m., at St. Cyprian's Episcopal Church, Tremont and Walpole Sts., of which Rev. Nathan Wright, Jr., is rector, there will be a memorial service in honor of the late Mrs. Ethel Paine Raven, who was a benefactress of the Urban League of Greater Boston and who financially assisted many Negro students in obtaining higher education. Better known as Mrs. John F. Moors, the philanthropist married Canon Charles E. Raven of Cambridge, England, chaplain to Queen Elizabeth II, after her widowhood. She was the sister of Rev. George L. Paine, honorary president of the Boston NAACP Branch and long time executive secretary of the Boston Council of Churches, who is expected to be present.

The service is being sponsored by the Boston Chronicle staff. All organizations are invited to send representatives, who will be seated in special pews. Fr. Wright will preach the sermon.

Senate Resolve Hails Decision

This past week the Massachusetts Senate passed a Resolve to Congratulate the Supreme Court of the United States for its recent historic decision against educational segregation in the schools of America. The Resolve was passed unanimously and sent along to Washington. It was proposed and filed by Senator Daniel Rudsten of Dorchester, Senator Charles J. Innes of Boston and Senator John F. Collins of Roxbury.

Dr. William Worthy Laid To Rest

Flanked by the alumni of his alma mater, Lincoln University, Pa., the casket of the late Dr. William Worthy rolled slowly down the aisle of the old Charles St. Church, Mt. Vernon St., at the termination of funeral services on Monday, May 24.

The services were conducted by Rev. Daniel L. Laviscount of St. Mark Congregational Church, with Dr. G. Lake Imes of Baltimore, Md., and former chaplain at Tuskegee Institute, as eulogist. Dr. Imes was a classmate and life-long friend of Dr. Worthy. He had been requested by the late doctor to perform this particular duty at his demise.

Prominent among the mourners who thronged the church were Hon. James M. Curley, former governor of Massachusetts and several times Mayor of Boston; members of the medical and legal fraternities, among the latter being Atty. John W. Schenck of Boston, an alumnus of Lincoln.

The body laid in state for three hours preceding the service, at which Mrs. Ella France Jones was soloist with Mrs. Gladys Perdue at the organ.

Dr. Worthy's immediate relatives are his wife, Mrs. Mabel Worthy; son, William, Jr.; daughters, Myrtle, Ruth and Mrs. Helen Holt of Springfield, Mass.; brother, Kenchon Worthy and sister, Mrs. Susie Zillmer, both of Forsyth, Ga.; nephews: Prof. Samuel Hubbard of Hubbard Training School, Forsyth, Pa., and Atty. Maceo W. Hubbard of the Dept. of Justice, Washington, D. C.
(Continued on page 4)

Grandsons of Emperor Haile Selassie who are attending Columbia University, New York, from which he will receive an honorary degree, are (left to right) Merid and Samson Beyene. Both youths studied at Brighton College, Brighton, England, before entering Columbia. They are the sons of the Ethiopian hero, Prince Desta Demtu, who lost his life during the Italian Fascist invasion of Ethiopia in 1937. Their mother is Princess Tenagne Worq, one of the Emperor's four daughters.

His Imperial Majesty, Emperor Haile Selassie I of Ethiopia, will visit Boston and vicinity for six hours next Thursday, June 3, as one lap of his tour of the United States, Canada, and Mexico.

The emperor and his entourage, including his granddaughter, Her Imperial Highness, the Princess Sybel Desta, Oxford University student, will fly to Boston from New York in the morning. He will be received by Mayor John B. Hynes and Governor Christian A. Herter.

Leader of his people in their struggle against Mussolini's invasion of their country in 1935, Emperor Haile Selassie was invited in 1944 by the late President D. Roosevelt to visit the United States, but was unable to come at that time. He arrived in New York last Monday aboard the liner "United States." Last Tuesday he was guest of President and Mrs. Dwight D. Eisenhower in the White House.

In Harlem Sunday Afternoon

Emperor Haile Selassie will be the special guest of Congressman Adam Clayton Powell, Jr., pastor of Abyssinia Baptist Church, Harlem, New York, at a ceremony in which he will be presented a specially bound history of the church, written by the late pastor-emeritus, Rev. Adam Clayton Powell, Sr. The church was founded in 1808 by free merchants from Abyssinia, as Ethiopia was then called. Police have made provisions for 50,000 persons outside the church edifice on 138th St.

In Cambridge At Noon

At noon on Thursday Emperor Haile Selassie will visit Massachusetts Hall, Harvard University, where he will meet President Nathan M. Pusey and other university officers before being conducted on a brief tour.

Mayor Hynes To Tender Luncheon

At the Hotel Sheraton Plaza in Copley Sq., at 1 p.m., Mayor Hynes will give a luncheon in honor of the emperor and his party, after which Governor Herter will do the honors at the State House. Since the legislature will be prorogued it is unlikely that the emperor will address the house of representa-
(Continued on page 5)

Deputy Director

WILFRED SCOTT, Republican leader of Ward 12, who is deputy director of the planning board of the State Club.

Boston Chronicle, May 29, 1954

Boston Chronicle

VOL. XXXIX, NO. 25   BOSTON, MASS., SATURDAY, JUNE 19, 1954   PRICE FIVE CENTS

See Page 12 For Week's Pictures

Square Named for War Hero

What Selassie Asked Bostonians

By William Harrison and Ernest E. Goodman

Now it can be told. A question asked of several Negro Bostonians who had the honor of conversing with His Imperial Majesty Emperor Haile Selassie of Ethiopia was: "Where are colored people?" He noted the relative fewness of their numbers at the city-state luncheon tendered him a the Hotel Sheraton Plaza, observed that the route taken by the motorcade did not go through any district similar to Harlem, where he had been cheered by 300,000 on the previous Sunday, and beamed on the less than baker's dozen who bade him farewell at the Logan Airport while he boarded a Canadian Royal Air Force transport.

The lie that the emperor sought to dissociate himself and his people from Negro Americans, despite the aid which they enthusiastically gave in time of Ethiopia's direst need (1935-36), was effectively countered by his remarks when he received the honorary degree of Doctor of Laws from Harvard University, Washington, on Friday, May 28. On that occasion the emperor said: "It is a curious fact, if we reflect upon it for a moment, that Africa has always exerted its influence and brought to bear its contribution in the West. It is certain that the United States of America would not have reached today its present world stature were it not, in part, for the enormous labours of Africans whose great descendants are here represented on this occasion."

The emperor said that the world is becoming increasingly aware of the importance of the contributions made by colored people to higher and broader standards of social concepts. Evidently referring to the recent Supreme Court decision outlawing segregation in the public schools, the Emperor declared, "Events of recent days, here in the United States, have brilliantly confirmed before the world the contributions which you have made to the principle that all men are brothers and equal in the sight of God."

In reference to Howard University, which was conferring its 147th honorary degree since the practice was started at the institution in 1874, the emperor affirmed, "You have reason to be proud of the role which you are (Continued on page 8)

(Continued on page 8)

Cambridge Lass Graduates

Miss Barbara Ann Williams, daughter of Mr. and Mrs. Harold H. Williams of Cambridge and West Yarmouth, graduated with honors from the Chandler School for Women as an Executive Secretary.

Miss Williams was very active in the school activities. She was a member of the Glee Club, played an important role in the Christmas Party given annually for over 200 children at the Robert Gould Shaw House, and was also voted Treasurer of the Senior Class.

At the present time, Miss Williams is affiliated with the Connick Associates as Secretary.

WANTED

Counselors, experienced or College students or entering college students accepted. Girls Camp 200 miles from Boston. Write stating qualifications, references, salary desired. Address: Miss Josephine Crawford 208 West Street, Canton, Mass.

William E. Dingwall
Attorney at Law
364 Mass. Ave., Boston, Mass.
KEnmore 6-9471

Ushers To Meet In Providence

The 10th annual convocation of the Interdenominational Ushers Association of New England, Inc., was held in Congdon St. Baptist Church, Providence, June 11, 12, 13. James Hall, of Boston, is president of the group.

The sessions of the Junior group were held on Saturday, June 12, at the Olney St. Baptist Church, with Sister Lillie B Williams, supervisor of the Junior Ushers, in charge.

Honorary Degree To Grant Still

Lewiston, Maine—At its annual commencement on Sunday Bates College conferred the honorary degree of Doctor of Letters upon William Grant, famous Negro composer of the "Afro-American Symphony."

Elected Chaplain

Cambridge, Mass.—Ulysses H. Gore of this city has been reelected chaplain of the Middlesex County Council, Veterans of Foreign Wars for a second term. He is past commander of Isaac W. Taylor Post, and heads that post's youth activities department.

Jimcrow Schools Ended In Panama Canal Zone

Washington — All segregation in schools operating in the Canal Zone will be ended in September, the Washington Bureau of the NAACP has been informed.

The government action to end present policies of excluding colored children was the subject of a complaint submitted last February to the Department of the Army by Clarence Mitchell, director of the Washington Bureau of the National Association for the Advancement of Colored People.

At that time, the NAACP pointed out that the existing segregation in the Canal Zone schools was contrary to policies established by President Eisenhower.

Robert D. King, Deputy Assistant Secretary of the Army, has now advised the Association that "effective at the beginning of the next semester, all U. S. citizens who reside in the Canal Zone and who are in the service of the United States Government will be admitted to any school operated by the Canal Zone Government. This is irrespective of race, creed, or color."

Scottish Rite Masons St. John's Day at Springfield

SPRINGFIELD, Mass.—Sunday, June 20, at 3 p.m., St. John's Day will be observed here with annual services at Mount Calvary Baptist Church, John St., of which Rev. Herbert S. Sumpter is pastor, by Most Worshipful Hiram Grand Lodge, Inc., A. F. and A. M., Jurisdiction of Massachusetts, under the leadership of Grand Master St. Clair Kirton of Boston. Special guests will be members of the Bay State Grand Chapter, Order of the Eastern Star.

Bostonians who intend to take part in the services may leave from buses which will leave 1024 Tremont St., Sunday morning, at 11 o'clock.

Radcliffe Honors Alumna, Senior

Cambridge, Mass. — At the dedication of the Helen Keller Garden of the propose Radcliffe Graduate Quadrangle last Saturday afternoon, in honor of the famous Helen Keller, Class of 1904, the Alumnae Achievement Award was presented by Mrs. Charles W. Phinney to Miss Keller and the Graduate Chapter Medal to Dr. Merze Tate, professor of history and International law at Howard University, Washington. The medal is awarded annually for distinguished scholarship and creative achievement in recognition of outstanding contributions of women who have received advanced (Continued on page 11)

(Continued on page 11)

HERO'S FAMILY RELAXES after dedication of the James R. Hodsdon, Jr., Square at Warwick and Hammond Sts. Roxbury, are (seated) left to right; Mrs. James R. Hodsdon, Sr., mother, Mrs. James R. Hodsdon, Jr., widow, James R. Hodsdon, Sr., father. Standing, left to right, are Miss Mary L. Hodson, sister, and Mrs. Mary E. Coles, aunt. (Photo by Ray Coleman)

Early Sunday afternoon traffic was impassable through Hammond and Warwick Sts., Roxbury, where a dense crowd numbering hundreds of his former neighbors and representatives of various veterans' organizations gathered to witness the ceremonies dedicating Lt. James R. Hodsdon, Jr., Square. Lt. Hodsdon was killed in Korea July 19, 1953, a few days before the truce, and the president efforts of his childhood friend, John G. Bynoe, past commander of Patrick E. Toy Post, Veterans of Foreign Wars, resulted in this commemoration of the hero.

Before the ceremonies the annual memorial services of veterans and civic organizations were held at Charles St. A.M.E. Church, Elm Hill Ave. and Warren St., Roxbury, of which Rev. Walter C. Davis is pastor. From the church the various groups paraded to the square, where Mr. Bynoe presided.

Dr. Silas F. "Shag" Taylor spoke briefly and eloquently on behalf of the bereaved family, and Mrs. Melnea Cass, state president of the United War Mothers of America, Inc., presented flowers from the community to Lt. Hodsdon's widow and mother. Rev. Fr. Joseph Keenan of St. Francis de Sales Church offered prayer.

Lt. Hodsdon was born in Roxbury, and was the son of James R. and Mary Hodsdon of 13 Warwick St., a house which faces the square which now bears his name. He attended the Boston public schools and Suffolk University before his induction (Continued On Page 9)

(Continued On Page 9)

St. John's Day Rite at Old North Church

Sunday afternoon, June 20, will occur the annual St. John's Day services of the Prince Hall Masons, Jurisdiction of Massachusetts.

Members of the order will assemble at the Robert Gould Shaw monument in front of the State House at 2:30 p.m., and will march from there, led by Grand Master Dr. James R. Lesueur, to the historic Old North Church, North End, in which meetings were held when Prince Hall founded Masonry in the 18th century. Bishop Northan B. Nash of the Protestant Episcopal Church, Diocese of Massachusetts, is rector, and Rev. Charles Russell Peck is Vicar. A special invitation was extended to the Prince Hall Masons to hold the services in the church. The observance will commemorate the 179th anniversary of the order's founding.

R. W. Cleo W. Wooten, Grand Secretary for Foreign Correspondence, will read the history of Prince Hall Masonry. Rev. Samuel L. Laviscount, pastor of St. Mark Congregational Church, Roxbury, will preach the sermon.

Guests of honor will be the Grand Lodge; Grand Chapter, Order of the Eastern Star, Jurisdiction of Massachusetts; Order of the Eastern Star, Jurisdiction of New England. R. W. Frederick J. Timberlake is chairman of the St. John's Day program committee.

Boston Chronicle, June 19, 1954

Call and Post

CITY EDITION
15 CENTS

Entered as 2nd Class Matter at Post Office, Cleveland, Ohio, under Act of March 8, 1879.

CLEVELAND, OHIO, SATURDAY, JUNE 12, 1954

4 Sections—Sec. 1—32 Pages 15c

BETTY BUTLER, for whom all legal possibilities have been exhausted in a sustained fight to save her from becoming the third Ohio woman to die in the electric chair.

IN RACE-HATE ATTACKS

PATROLS GUARD HOMES

'Press on', Selassie Tells U. S. Negroes

A MESSAGE FOR NEGRO AMERICANS

Emperor Praises Edict on Jim-Crow Schools

BY JAMES L. HICKS

OTTAWA, Canada— Emperor Haile Selassie told the people of Canada here Friday that he was happy the United States Supreme Court had outlawed segregated schools.

"The decision of the court is in keeping with the principles and ideals of the United States Constitution," the Emperor said.

The statement came as the plane when it arrived in Boston Emperor and his party of 24 to pick up the Emperor.

Sends Message of Courage to Negro Citizens

BY JAMES L. HICKS

NEW YORK, N. Y. — Emperor Haile Selassie Wednesday advised the colored people...

Cleveland Call and Post, June 12, 1954

109

Lion Of Judah Conquers The Windy City

Emperor Haile Selassie of Ethiopia arrived in Chicago Monday evening and after a 24-hour visit and tour, the Conquering Lion of Judah departed, on his way to St. Paul where he was scheduled to spend the next two days.

The Emperor, accompanied by his huge entourage, including his third son and a granddaughter, toured the city in style. The tour included a train ride to the Burlington roundhouse in Cicero, Ill., a visit to the world's largest stockyards, a steel mill and meat packing center.

He was also honored at a luncheon Tuesday, sponsored by the Chicago Association of Commerce and Industry and attended by approximately 1,200 persons.

Chicago Defender, June, 1954

Emperor Selassie Links Negro With Africans Throughout World

Emperor Haile Selassie extended his whirlwind tour of Chicago Tuesday when he made an unscheduled stop at the South Park Baptist church and made perhaps the most significant speech of his tour here.

The Emperor majestically poised on the rostrum of the church, told some 3,000 persons that if the United States has been able to assume its outstanding position as leader in the world today, "it has been due, in no small part, to your profound religious faith and ideals.

"The high station which the United States has attained has also been due to the devoted labours of every American citizen. And not the least of the credit for these achievements is due to the numerous groups of American citizens who have made their home on the great African continent of which Ethiopia is proud to be a part."

Recalling his 1936 warning to the League of Nations, when Italy was invading his country, Selassie said that in those "difficult hours in our fight for independence, we were not standing alone because peoples of African origin throughout the world were with us in spirit through their moral and spiritual support.

"It is only natural, therefore," he continued," that we Africans should follow with deepest interest the inspiring achievements and contributions of the peoples of African origin in the United States. By your actions, your devotions and your sacrifices you are justifying throughout the world the advancement of the cause of racial and social equality and the right of all peoples to freedom,

FULL DRESS TREATMENT was the order of the day for Emperor Haile Selassie during his visit in Chicago. Here little ruler stands surrounded by police captain and detail of officers all drawn up to full salute in honor of his majesty.

independence and self-expression."

South Park Baptist church has a membership of 875, but more than 3,000 persons had jammed the church and street 45 minutes before the Emperor and his party arrived. Only several hours before the appearance he notified security agents and his Chief of Protocol, Endalkatchew Makonnen, that he was going to extend his tour and visit the church.

He was scheduled to arrive at the church at 5 p. m. One hour earlier he had left the United States works in South Chicago, went back to the Drake hotel for a short rest and was then at the church at the designated time.

As the Emperor arpproached the church the student band of Wendell Phillips High school was playing the Star Spangled Banner. Mrs. Virginia Lewis, principal of the school, welcomes the emperor on behalf of Southside schools.

O. F. Douglas, prominent Baptist layman and sponsor of the

Religious Radio Announcers' Guild, headed to committee arranging the Emperor's visit to the Southside. Cooperating with Douglas was Winston Evans, secretary of the Ethiopian World Federation, Inc.

General Richard Jones of South Center department store, extended a welcome in behalf of the area businessmen and Rev. E. Williams, who was later awarded the Star of Ethiopia medal, presented the Conquering Lion of Judah.

The Emperor, who had said that he was "deeply moved" by the church gathering, possessed one of his rare smiles as he left the church, shaking hands with enthusiastic onlookers as he passed them on the way to his waiting $35,000 bullet-proofed limousine.

The Emperor's speech before the church gathering refuted, as he did in Washington and New York, rumors that he and his people did not want to be identified with American Negroes.

Churchmen Shun Texas Over Bias

NEW YORK — Plans to hold the 1955 convention of the Protestant Episcopal church in Houston, Tex., were canceled this week because some churchmen had opposed that city on grounds of racial segregation policies there.

In announcing the decision, the Rt. Rev. Henry Knox Sherrill, presiding bishop of the church, made no mention of the segregation question. But a church spokesman said, however, that was the reason for the change in plans.

Chicago Defender, June, 1954

Ethiopian Emperor Is Chicago's King For A Day

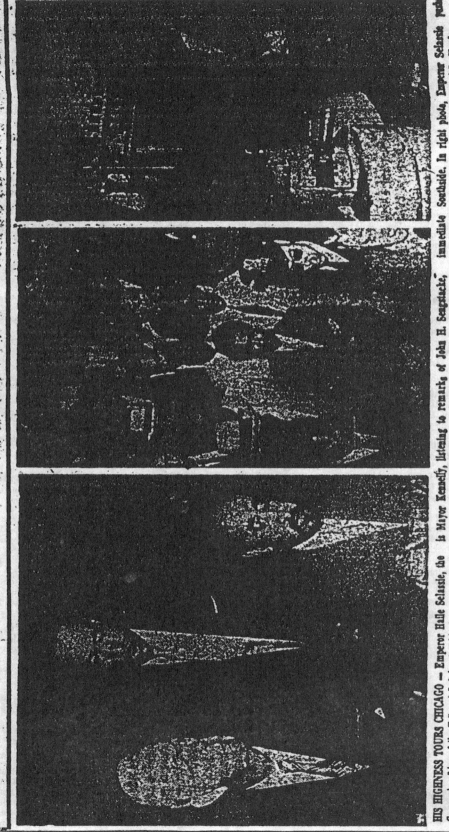

HIS HIGHNESS TOURS CHICAGO — Emperor Haile Selassie, the Conquering Lion of the Tribe of Judah, of Ethiopia, conquered all Chicago during his feverish-paced tour last week. Left photo shows Emperor at luncheon at Sherman Hotel. Seated next to Selassie is Mayor Kennelly, listening to remarks of John H. Sengstacke, editor and publisher of the Chicago Defender. Center photo shows Emperor Selassie being escorted through crowd at South Park Baptist church, his only appearance, though unscheduled, in the immediate Southside. In right photo, Emperor Selassie pulled throttle of diesel engine on way to Clearn Freight Yards.

Defender photos by Rhoden

Chicago Defender, June, 1954

Selassie's Special Message For Negroes

By JAMES L. HICKS

NEW YORK—Emperor Haile Selassie Wednesday advised the colored people of the United States to continue to press their social and intellectual advancement forward "with Christian courage" and to be confident that justice and equality will eventually triumph throughout the world.

The direct message to Negro Americans was given by the Emperor in the first exclusive interview he has granted since arriving here May 25.

The message came after this reporter had informed the Emperor's staff that there was confusion in the minds of colored Americans as to the Emperor's position on the racial question and asked the Emperor directly if he had a message for the colored people of America.

The Emperor's direct reply to this reporter's question was:

"My message to the colored people of the United States is that they continue to press forward with determination, their social and intellectual advancement, meeting all obstacles with Christian courage and toler-

ance, confident in the certainty of the eventual triumph of justice and equality throughout the world."

During the brief but exclusive interview the Emperor also exploded the oft repeated rumor that the people of Ethiopia do not wish to be identified with the colored people of America or associate themselves with their problems.

With this rumor in mind I asked the Emperor this question:

KINDRED FEELING

"Is there a kindred feeling between your people and the colored people of America."

The Emperor replied: "The people of Ethiopia feel the strongest bond of sympathy and understanding with the colored people of the United States. We greatly admire your achievements and your contributions to American life and the tremendous development of this great nation."

"I have," the Emperor said, "been deeply impressed with the warmth of the reception which the colored people of the United States have reserved for me."

See SELASSIE — Page 2, Col. 3

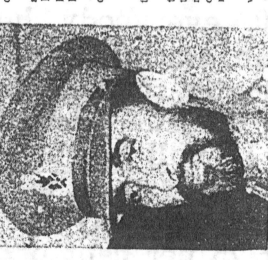

HAILE SELASSIE

THIS PAPER CONSISTS OF TWO PARTS — PART ONE

Chicago Defender

WORLD'S GREATEST WEEKLY

NATIONAL

Copyright 1954 by the Robert S. Abbott Pub. Co., 3435 Indiana Ave., CAlumet 5-5656

CHICAGO, ILLINOIS—SATURDAY, JUNE 12, 1954

50th YEAR OF PUBLICATION

VOL. L—No. 6

Cops Guard Two; Fear Digit War

Eclipse of Sun Next Wednesday

Mother Nature is planning a dramatic spectacle next Wednesday, June 30, everybody hearabouts with an alarm clock and a piece of heavily smoked glass. An eclipse of the sun, visible in New England, will occur between 6:07 and 8:07 a. m. At about 7 o'clock, midway in the eclipse, about 75 per cent of the sun's disc will be obscured for Yankee viewers by the moon passing between the sun and the earth, according to John Patterson, director of the Hayden Planetarium at Boston's new Museum of Science.

Boston Chronicle, June 26, 1954

114

Asks U. S. Court Ban on Travel Jim Cro

SECTION--C
EDITORIALS

Cleveland
Call and Post
Ohio's Finest Growing Weekly
Second Front Page

National News
SPORTS

**Blow For Fre
Urged By Ci
Liberties Un**

SATURDAY, JUNE 26, 1954

★★ PAGE ONE—C

Haile Spends 2 Days in Okla.

Unconscious of New Experiment In U. S. Education

By CHAS. H. LOEB, for NNPA

STILLWATER, Okla. — Wined and dined as befits royalty by the elite of Oklahoma, Emperor Haile Selassie of Ethiopia spent two days here last week completely unconscious that right between the royal feet of his royal party a new experiment in American education was taking place.

The event is the hesitant, almost tortuous program which A & M College authorities have hit upon as the best method of complying with the edict of the U. S. Supreme Court outlawing segregation in the tax-supported schools of the nation.

There are about 300 Negro students attending summer classes on the A & M campus. They are marvelling over the completely unrestrained reception this colored monarch has been accorded by college officials they have heard state sincerely that "the time is not yet ripe for the admission of a Negro undergraduate student to our student dormitories."

Nothing Strange

During this reporter's stay not a single white person with whom I have come into contact has given

Attend Ohioans Graduation

CLARK COLLEGE GRADUATE—Yvonne Southall is shown with her family and Clark President, Dr. James B. Brawley, following the college commencement exercises in Davage Auditorium. Miss Southall, who assisted with typing instruction at the college, is a native of East Liverpool, Ohio. Pictured from left: Mrs. M. A. Scott Sr., her aunt, Atlanta, Ga.; Mrs. Anna Perry, School Circle, Ga.; Miss Southall; her mother, Mrs. Irene Southall, East Liverpool; Dr. William Southall, he father, and Mrs. Georgie Banks, an aunt, also of East Liverpool, Ohio.

At Jackson - Jefferson Dinner

Discrimination Unintentional: Steamship Line

NEW YORK — Apologizing for the segregation of a Negro passenger in the dining room of the S. S. Queen of Bermuda, J. J. Walsh, local director of Furness, Withy & Co., owners of the liner, has assured the National Association for the Advancement of Colored People that "there was no intention of discrimination."

Upon complaint of Mrs. M. Josephine Wooten, New York school teacher, Mr. White wrote to the steamship company. On a trip to Bermuda last summer, Mrs. Wooten charges that she was set apart from other passengers and assigned to a table alone in the dining room.

Mr. Walsh assured the NAACP executive that "it is not our policy to discriminate against anyone due to race, color or creed." Employees of the company are, he said, "instructed to be as tactful as possible but it might appear that in this instance there was a slipup and we are sorry that the party in question was displeased."

WASHINGTON, D. C.
The American Civil Libe Monday urged Congress a major blow for fre barring segregation in railroads engaged in commerce.

In a statement file House Interstate an Commerce Committee, gave its "unqualified su bill introduced by Rep John W. Heselton, Rep Massachusetts, allows denied equal treatmen state carriers to brin suits in Federal courts.

The ACLU said the cision of the Supreme hibiting segregation schools had paved the w gressional action stri other forms of discrim

The Supreme Court that segregation of inte sengers on buses place burden on commerce fore is unconstitutiona also ruled passengers ly be segregated in din railroads. But there a eral laws against the carriers have resorted devices to enforce s tion.

The ACLU statemen ACLU believes that should any government ed segregation or dis he struck down as a v the equal protection guaranteed by our C but that any manifesta regation or discrimina quasi-public agency suc mon carrier must and ended by legislative ac

Begin Pastor's S
GREENSBORO, N
Pastor's School of the Area, The Methodist C gan its annual three sion at Bennett College

Probe of Racial

Haile Selassie Meets State Officials, Ir

JOSTLING EACH OTHER good naturedly, Negro and white citizens of Oklahoma waited behind a chain link barrier to get a glimpse of Emperor Haile Selassie when his plane landed for the first stop on his tour of the South. Waiting crowd is seen in first panel.

In second panel, Emperor is met by high officials of Oklahoma and Oklahoma A&M College. Left to right in second panel are Dr. A.

E. Darlow, dean of A&M department of agriculture; Governor Ja E. Berry, Dr. Oliver S. Wilhelm, president of Oklahoma A&M; Emperor, and a State Department aide.

In third panel Princess Sebla Desta (left) and Prince Sahle S sie, Haile Selassie, the Emperor's grandson (third from left ho

SELASSIE SIDELIGHTS:

Emperor Smiles as Indian Chief Adds New Name

By CHARLES H. LOEB for NNPA

STILLWATER, Okla. — Emperor Selassie, who had not seen a native American Indian during his entire tour, had a wish fulfilled at Stillwater. Acee Blue Eagle, a Pawnee Indian artist and former student at Oxford, wearing a full head-dress and buckskin clothing, presented the Emperor with a Pawnee war bonnet and gave him the name Great Buffalo High Chief. In similar presentations to the emperor's third son, 23-year-old Prince Sahle Selassie Haile Selassie, and grand-daughter, Princess Sebla Desta, he conferred the names "Thunder Eagle" and "Morning Star" respectively.

The Indian evoked from the dead-pan Emperor his most genuine smile of the Oklahoma trip. Throughout the exciting social fanfare attending his visit he maintained the most perfect expression of complete boredom I have ever witnessed.

—o—

Omnibus Civil Rights Measure Is Introduced

New Orleans Planning N

SECTION--C
EDITORIALS

CLEVELAND
Call and Post
Ohio's Fastest Growing Weekly
Second Front Page

SATURDAY, JULY 3, 1954

U.S. Court Bans Jimcrow Public

Clevelan
Southern

'Integration Will Make Such Misunderstanding a Thing of the Past'

THE SOUTH

WHITE

NEGRO

UNCLE SAM

Why Haile Selassie Planned Visit To Stillwater, Okla.

By CHAS. H. LOEB for NNPA

STILLWATER, Okla. (NNPA)— It was no imperial whim that caused his Imperial Majesty Haile Selassie I, of Ethiopia, to choose Stillwater and Oklahoma Agricultural and Mechanical College as the only stop on a flight from California to Mexico. The practical little Emperor wanted a first-hand look at the institution upon which he is modeling his own nation's agricultural and mechanical institutions.

The story behind the Emperor's real purpose in stopping off here for two inspection and reception-filled half-days, was told to me by Miss Marie Berger, an intense, fast-talking career woman who heads the East Africa Branch of the Foreign Operations Administration.

It all began when the late Dr. Henry Garland Bennett, former president of A & M visited Ethiopia about three years ago. He was immediately impressed by the country's extremely rich soil (rich and black) and favorable climate (like Southern California). Bennett met and talked with Emperor Selassie and later became his agricultural advisor.

When President Truman's Point Four program reached Ethiopia about three years ago, emphasis was placed on agricultural development. The Point Four administration contracted with Oklahoma A & M to supply agricultural experts to train Ethiopians in scientific agricultural know-how.

A & M Experts Sought

Since that time, these A & M experts have made appreciable progress in getting Ethiopia's agricultural development well under way. According to Miss Berger, there are now 35 A & M people stationed in the little African kingdom. Top ranking among them is Dr. Luther H. Brannon, former assistant director of agricultural extension at A & M who is now president of the new Ethiopian A & M College. Brannon also heads the country's agricultural development projects.

While his Ethiopian colleges and schools are training native teachers to take over the work of research and education, Emperor Selassie also has his eye open for good American schools in which to train Ethiopian students.

There was one Ethiopian student on the A & M campus here last year, who completed a special course in agriculture, attended regular classes, was assigned to the regular dormitories without even a raised eyebrow from white students. His only embarrassment came on the infrequent trips he made into the town of Stillwater and was mistaken by one of its colored citizens as "one of us."

During his visit here, the Emperor spent much more time inspecting the barns than he did the ballrooms.

LOUIS LAUTIER IN THE Nation's Capital

WASHINGTON—Unless general opposition to further amendment of the Constitution arises, it appears that this Congress will pass a resolution proposing an amendment to outlaw the poll tax. Only five states—Virginia, Alabama, Arkansas, Mississippi and Texas now have laws requiring the payment of a poll tax as a condition for voting.

Ten Senators from Southern States (two of them are now deceased) are sponsoring a resolution to abolish the poll tax and forbid the imposition of any tax or property qualification as a condition for voting in Federal elections.

Senator William Langer, of North Dakota, chairman of the Senate Judiciary Committee, after listening to exhaustive testimony from Senator Spessard L. Holland, Democrat, of Florida, promised that his committee would report the resolution promptly.

Under the sponsorship of southern Senators, the resolution, if reported from committee, will not run into a filibuster.

Since 1939, according to the Congressional Library Legislative Reference Service, 119 anti-poll tax bills have been introduced. Every time one of these bills has been called up for Senate consideration, it has been filibustered to death.

In opposing such bills, southern Senators have

stitutional amendment to abolish the poll tax has melted away. There remains the other question of the probability of speedy adoption of the proposed amendment.

Senator Holland feels very strongly that ratification can be speedily accomplished. He points out that five Southern States ratified the Seventeenth Amendment (including Louisiana which was the thirty-seventh state to ratify).

The amendment, providing for the election of Senators by popular vote, was ratified so promptly that complete ratification was accomplished in eleven months from the date of submission.

Senator Holland pledged that each of the sponsors of the resolution will use his best endeavors in his state to accomplish speedy ratification of the amendment.

The one thing which may prove a stumbling block to passage of the Holland resolution at this session of Congress may be the amendment sponsored by Senator John M. Butler, Republican, of Maryland, intended chiefly to prevent the packing of the Supreme Court.

This amendment would restrict the number of judges to nine and compel retirement of all Federal judges at the age of 75 years.

Objections do not run so much as to the merits of this amendment as they do to the question of

---

people today
desegregation
political, social

if we are
at is so new
ing difficulty

oped up for
do the things
which it was
ly release it,
adjusting it-
ngs will have
to learn how
ct itself from

rced to go to
deliberately
anly possible
living in the
conveniences
ly with; kept
playgrounds;
h institutions
ab at the low-
by the peace
justice in all
and many
is of years of
second class
ve formed the
the United

ra of desegre-
to do? How
Will we be
emies?

we, too, are
ength. We are
o use muscles
efore. We are
some pleasant

uture ahead of
road to travel
s journey suc-
evertheless, is

Washington,
anta School of
vice when he
ad teachers to
tudents as the
egration. He
our own insti-
egration.

to be a point
inking. Take a

CHUCKLES FROM THE AIRWAVES

ETHIOPIAN EMPEROR INVADES THE SOUTH

CALLS FOR FULL EQUALITY

By CHARLES H. LOEB

NEW ORLEANS (NNPA)—Speaking to nearly 3,000 citizens in a public address on the campus of Dillard University here Thursday, Emperor Haïle Selassie reemphasized his strong belief in full equality in human relations.

It was the Emperor's only public speech during his whirlwind visit to the Crescent City, and his second emphatic reassertion of the principles of equality.

In answer to a direct question at his City Hall press conference two hours earlier, he had said the United States Supreme Court had acted with great wisdom in outlawing public school segregation and that he felt the decision would go a long way towards enhancing American ideals in the mind of "people everywhere."

(Continued on PAGE TWO A)

CITY EDITION

CLEVELAND Call and Post

Ohio's Fastest Growing Weekly

Entered as 2nd Class Matter at Post Office, Cleveland, Ohio, under Act of March 8, 1879

VOL. 49—NO. 23   CLEVELAND, OHIO, SATURDAY, JULY 3, 1954   4 Sec.—36 Pages—Sec

MAN, WOMAN DIE

Cleveland Call and Post, July 3, 1954

118

Emperor Dines with Governor Aboard Yacht, Visits Loyola University

—Photos by The Times-Picayune.

PONDERING A CHOICE of foods during a buffet lunch Friday aboard the yacht Good Neighbor, Emperor Haile Selassie of Ethiopia precedes Gov. Robert F. Kennon past the array of dishes. At right, the emperor is welcomed to Loyola university by Archbishop Joseph Francis Rummel. In the foreground (from left) are the archbishop; the Rev. W. Patrick Donnelly, university president; Mayor deLesseps S. Morrison, and Emperor Selassie.

Selassie Hopes Big Powers Will Heed Peace Yearning

Emperor and Entourage End Two-Day Visit

Haile Selassie I said Friday that hopes for world peace may continue if the major powers will listen to the pleas of the smaller nations.

In an interview, the emperor of Ethiopia said, "If the collective security is strong and if the smaller governments are heard by the General Assembly (in the United Nations), the peace will be surer."

His remarks were made during the second day of his two-day visit to New Orleans. The Selassie entourage left the city at 4:18 p. m. for Ft. Benning, Ga., by chartered plane.

In the interview conducted in French aboard the yacht Good Neighbor, the bearded monarch declined to state definitely wh...

tive Amharic tongue, his words being translated in English by a staff interpreter.

Gets 21-Gun Salute

Also accompanying the monarch on his trip and tour were a son, His Imperial Highness Prince Sahle Selassie Haile Selassie, 23, and two granddaughters, Her Highness Princess Sebla Desta, 23, and Her Highness Princess Sofia Desta, 20.

As the yacht passed the Algiers Naval Station, the king received a 21-gun salute as the station's personnel, dressed in white, lined the decks of four ships at the wharf. Standing at the emperor's side was Rear Admiral John M. Higgins, commandant of the Eighth Naval District.

A member of Emperor Selassie's staff identified Gov. Kennon's decoration as the Grand

SYNAGOGUE TO FETE 67TH ANNIVERSARY

Chevra Thilim Synagogue will hold its 67th anniversary supper dance Sunday at 8:30 p. m. at the St. Charles hotel.

The theme of the event will emphasize the new synagogue building, constructed five years ago, and the birthday cake will have five candles instead of 67 for that reason.

Two pictures contrasting the old and new synagogues, painted by Molly Gordon, will form the stage backdrop.

The musical portion of the program will range from traditional Jewish ballards to modern music via the barbership quartet.

SUNDAY TO BE 'MEN'S DAY'

Sunday will be "Men's Day" at Mt. Calvary Christian Methodist Episcopal church, 3621 Dryades, Rev. E. L. Johnson, pastor, announced. Rev. C. C. Petiford, Bastrop, presiding elder of the New Orleans district, will deliver the address.

It's Yours For On... $10 DOWN and...

New York Times, June 26, 1954

Haile Selassie Honors Rogers

NEW YORK—Just prior to his departure for France Emperor Haile Selassie I of Ethopia summoned J. A. Rogers, famous historian to his Waldorf-Astoria suite, where Mr. Rogers was presented a gold medal given an order for 128 copies of his book, World's Great Men of Color, 3000 B. C. to 1946 A. D.

After the presentation Mr. Rogers stated: "This ought to squelch the belief held by some that he considers himself white and is not intrested in colored Americans." He continued: "I first met him at his coronation in 1930. At 61 the emperor is in excellent health. He underwent a physical examination at Harkness Pavilion of the Presbyterian Hospital and passed with flying colors."

Boston Daily Globe 1954

Our Opinions

Hail Haile Selassie

Several weeks ago, just before his arrival here, we wrote an editorial and captioned it: "A Memo to Selassie."

We don't know whether he saw it, but we are glad to note that the Emperor is making friends and influencing people in the United States.

Our earlier editorial reflected the concern of especially Negroes in this country over reports that the Emperor did not wish to be identified with American Negroes.

Those who have followed his visits to New York City Washington and Chicago report that he has gone out of his way to demonstrate his identity with the American Negro.

In New York City, he made a special trip to Harlem, worshipped at Abyssinian Baptist church, after attending services at the Greek Orthodox church of his own faith.

In Washington, he visited the campus of Howard university where he was awarded an honorary degree. A part of his remarks on that occasion was addressed to the descendants of African people.

Later in an interview in New York, he issued a special message to the American Negroes which was carried on the front page of this paper last week.

In Chicago, last week, he made room on his already crowded itinerary to include a stop at South Park Baptist church where 3,000 Southsiders greeted him with unbounded enthusiasm.

George Daniels, Defender reporter who traveled with the Emperor's party during the Chicago visit reported that Haile Selassie's countenance brightened when his car pulled up at the church and a wildly enthusiastic crowd greeted him.

Daniels believes it was the high point of the day for the Emperor.

In New York, he cited James R. Lawson, president of the United African Nationalist movement, who had been snubbed by the official welcoming committee.

In Chicago he decorated Janet Harmon former aviatrix and long friend of Ethiopia.

An Irish policeman in Chicago described the Emperor as "the king of the colored people."

At the rate he's going, he'll be just that to those who have followed his tour in the United States.

Chicago Defender, June, 1954

121

Jobs Go Begging, So Ethiopia Must Add Other Inducements

There are jobs looking for people in Ethiopia.

Jobs with these advantages — a house, rent-free, a salary at least equalling that which applicants are now earning or could earn in America, free transportation to Ethiopia for applicants and their families, annual three-month vacations with pay and — in some instances — automobiles provided by the government.

Details of these inviting employment situations were revealed to the DEFENDER this week by Madame Seth Sahara, Ethiopian business woman who is winding up an 18-month tour of America in search of technical aid in the task of rebuilding her country.

A personal emissary of Emperor Haile Selassie, Madame Sahara said there are openings for teachers, brick masons, electricians, tailors, beauty culturists, civil engineers, nurses, scientific farmers (to raise chickens and improve cattle breeds) as well as other tradesmen and professionals.

Madame Sahara, an earnest, pleasant woman, stressed the desire of the Ethiopian government to have colored Americans avail themselves of these positions.

She said there are a thousand Europeans to every single American Negro taking advantage of the employment opportunities in the Ethiopian capital, Addis Ababa and fifty-two other provinces in the country.

Among the inducements offered are transportation paid back and forth on vacation trips.

Contrary to most opinion, Madame Sahara said, climate in Ethiophia is not unpleasant. There is a spring-type climate the year around, she stated, with a six-month rainy season during which it rains half a day, either during the mornings or afternoons.

Americans who have an idea that Ethiopia is a jungle wild would be pleasantly surprised to find that Addis Ababa is an extremely modern city, she declared.

Persons interested in applying for employment in Ethiopia or receiving additional information are advised to write the Ethiopian Embassy in Washington.

Business opportunities are ripe in Ethiopia also, Madame Sahara said. Her government welcomes and will cooperate with persons with capital interested in setting up businesses. As an example of a successful experiment in this di-

VISITING DEFENDER OFFICES, Madame Seth Sahara displays monkey skins and mink rugs hand made by Ethiopian boy and girl students. A personal emissary of Emperor Haile Selassie, Madame Sahara has spent eighteen months in America spreading the word that employment opportunities are open for Americans in Ethiopia's rebuilding program. Left to right are Carter, Madame Sahara's husband, F. H. Hammurabi, research director of Friends of Africa, Inc., and Madame Sahara. Defender photo.

rection, the Ethiopian emissary cited Mrs. Mignant Ford, an American Negro who operates a private boarding school, established with her own funds but operating in a building provided rent-free by the government.

Beauticians, for example, would be particularly welcomed, Madame Sahara said. She revealed that in a city of 400,000 there are only two beauticians — both of them male Greeks. There is a good opportunity for cleaning, pressing and fowl-raising.

Accompanied by her husband, Clarence Carter, Madame Sahara has visited New York, Pennsylvania, Washington, Virginia, North Carolina, Florida, Georgia, Alabama, Tennessee, Kentucky, Ohio and Illinois, speaking at various colleges and public meetings.

In Tampa she had a friendly visit with Mrs. Mary Bethune, who has invited her to become an honorary life member of the National Council of Negro Women.

Mrs. Bethune's college, along with Florida Normal and Industrial Memorial College granted full scholarships for Ethiopian students as a result of Madame Sahara's missionary work.

Spanish Say Africans Are 'Babies'

SANTA ISABEL, Spanish G— —The African here, in the of the Spanish, are children must be taught and supervise til they can show that the capable of looking out and for themselves and families.

Here, as probably on no island, the African is shelter a baby and has a legal statu ilar to that of a minor.

On the Spanish island of nando Po, of which Santa Is the capital, the Spanish au ties have carried paternali its ultimate expression.

Santa Isabel, which is al capital of Spanish Guinea, l of old Spain slightly co round the edges by the cont tropical Africa.

The cocoa grown on Fa Po is second to none for q

Plantations are worked f most part by imported lab cruited from Nigeria on shor contract.

The African planters ar erally descendants of immi from Liberia or Sierra Leon some of them have achiev itions of wealth and infl But the vast majority of th cans here are still very ward.

A "non-emancipated" has a legal status similar of a minor. The parental f is performed by a board the Patronato de Indigenas.

The Patronato was sta 1927 primarily to prevent enation of African lands. N emancipated" African can rent his land, contract a more than 2,000 pesetas buy spirits without per from the Patronato.

The ultimate aim of this is to bring the African point where he can gover self on the individual, fam village level. The African to come under the Pa when he achieves full em tion by either earning a ba reate degree or by satisfyi Patronato of his maturity i other way.

MRS. LOYCE YOUNG DANIELS, of Meridian, Miss., daughter of the late E. F. Young, Jr., and Mrs. Velma Beale Young attended the Phi Chi Omega sorority convention in New York before sailing for

Albert BARNETT
News Headlines Overshadow Gains Made On The Race Relations Front

"SCARE" HEADLINES IN THE PUBLIC PRESS the past week were nation-wide in scope a n d touched upon a variety of interesting subjects, among them the following: The tense situation in Indo-China, relieved somewhat b y the statement of Rep. Judd (R.-Minn.) who said the administration has promised to ask per-

Association, it was learned last week. Dr. Free Strain, president of the Memphis group, said a committee has been named to "exploit all questions of professional and scientific affiliation" of Negro physicians at the county, state and AME levels.

The proposal to admit Negro medics came from Dr. John E.

Homecoming Planned For Army Medic

MERIDIAN, Miss. — C and civic organizations he planning a home-coming

Chicago Defender, May 1, 1954

FOREIGN NEWS

Dark Clouds Surround Lofty UN Headquarters

BY FRED SPARKS
Post Special Writer

UNITED NATIONS, N. Y., June 1—"Have you come to cover the funeral of the United Nations?"

So spoke a friend as I entered UN headquarters in Manhattan. His gloom clouds every corridor in this modernistic glass pile built to house a brave new world in which justice would wield the only sword.

For now the diplomats play in Geneva the ancient game of power politics, tanks and planes are the cards—the Communists bet Dien Bien Phu and the French pass.

The UN as a meeting hall for peace is ignored by the contestants at Geneva, as it was ignored at last winter's Berlin conference. The three terrible issues of today—Korea, Indo-

china, Germany—are out of UN hands. No wonder the talk of "funeral." The UN is being snubbed to death.

TEN YEARS ago Winston Churchill was taking a bath in the White House when Franklin Roosevelt, elated over victories in the West, called through the door: "How about naming it 'United Nations'?"

Churchill agreed. And thus a tag was created for the organization that lifted the hopes of billions—of white, black, brown and yellow peoples—and then drowned their hopes in a sea of words; words without deeds.

Ten years ago the politicians of the world spoke of a "new court of justice." And so the little people came for their day in court.

There was the intellectual

Czech who told of police clubs that beat the freedom out of his country.

THERE WAS the man with skin like polished black tile who wanted to know why his African tribesmen could not walk the main streets of their own cities.

There was the hollow-eyed Ukrainian woman who thought something should be done for the 10 million shuffling shadows in the slave camps of the Soviet Union.

They came . . . and then they went home without results, broken, bitter, having learned that the old law of life had not been repealed: power still owns justice, might makes right.

IN THE WAKE of this disillusion, has come a strange and often insane hatred. Match books are circulated in New York stamped with: "Get the UN out of the U. S.—and the U. S. out of the UN." Citizens who have seen so much of killing crowds the square of Seoul to chant: "The UN has sold us out."

In the eerie light of a jungle campfire Mau Maus swear a blood oath as their leader cries: "We can expect nothing from the UN—it is the tool of our oppressor." In the shabby tent camps of the Moslem refugees next the old city of Jerusalem two men with red fezzes, sluggish from a meager diet, post a sign lettered in shaky Arabic: "Remember the UN—it helped steal your home."

SUPPORTERS of the United Nations insist these people have expected too much—at least they have a forum. For example, there have been appeals for mistreated South African minorities. UN has done nothing.

But spokesmen for the oppressed have embarrassed South African and improvements—ever so slight have been made by the government itself. They argue: Publicity is a UN weapon.

But while the Soviet Press plays up weaknesses in the Free World, the Communists cannot be "embarrassed" by bad publicity at home. In their half of the earth censors have taken the old line "No news is good news" and added "for communism."

HOWEVER, those who plead for the UN say it has forced Soviet diplomates to operate on a global stage. Their arrogant performance has offended millions in a free world audience who — 10 years ago — thought they were bearable.

Each "veto" shriek from the mouth of a Vishinsky does more to brand Russia "non-co-operative" than a million accusations by anti-Communist orators.

Even about this there are doubts. An American Legion representative writes: "We can expect nothing from the UN that will not serve the Soviet Union."

* * *

OPPONENTS FEEL the Soviets care not about bad publicity abroad—but are delighted to watch the Free World divide itself as we have on colonies, racial segregation, Israel vs Arabia, recognition of Red China, equal responsibilities in the Korean War. . . .

And two of our strongest hopes for the defense of Asia and Europe—Japan and West Germany—are impatient be-

cause they are denied admission.

So the debate continues. It is no longer on "How much good will the UN do?" but "Is the UN worthwhile?"

The American people, in a recent poll, approved continued membership in the UN by 85 per cent—but with equal agreement said they had little faith in the ability of the UN to solve specific problems.

LARGELY RESPONSIBLE for today's global gloom are the politicians of 1944 who treated UN with the same glib carelessness they treat local issues. They did not bother to realize that while a campaign for votes is soon forgotten — the campaign for peace is eternal. They

overlooked history—and oversold UN.

In a frank survey, the UN secretary general, realistic Norwegian Dag Hammarskjold, says: "There was a widespread illusion (10 years ago) that UN would be able to enforce peace and impose the settlement of political disputes. This illusion has, of course, been thoroughly shattered."

And the chief U. S. delegate to UN, Henry Cabot Lodge, remarked: "The UN was not created in order to bring us to heaven, but in order to save us from hell."

(TOMORROW: Generals without an army.)

UNITED NATIONS HEADQUARTERS, NEW YORK
. . . ignored by big-power contestants

ANDREI VISHINSKY (LEFT) AND JACO MALIK
. . . arrogance for all the world to see

Cincinnati Post June 1, 1954

Saturday, June 19, 1954

Month of June is To offer Sky Gazers Celestial Phenomena

By Chales A. Isaac.

To those who have the leisure and the leaning to watch the wonders of the wide, blue sky, this month of June has two important events to offer. One is the Total Solar Eclipse, which occurs on June 30, and the other is the closest approach of Mars to the Earth.

A Solar Eclipse occurs when the New Moon comes between the Sun and the Earth, thus obscuring the former, either partially or totally, from the latter. A total eclipse is rather a rare phenomenon, while partial eclipses are much more common. Usually, a total eclipse does not continue for more than a few minutes. This year, in Ethiopia, the Solar Eclipse is expected to begin around Noon on Wednesday, June 30, and go on until late in the afternoon.

Since the Big Rains have begun early this year, the sky is generally overcast with clouds, which are likely to rob the observers of the pleasure of watching a very interesting celestial phenomenon. Even if the sky remains cloudless, observers in all parts of Ethiopia (say, in such remote parts as Sidamo is from Tigre) may not see the eclipse in its total state. Nevertheless, they will see the greater portion of the Sun's light cut off by the intervening New Moon.

Mars, the most controversial of all planets, can be seen nowadays between the constellations of Sagittarius and Scorpius. It can be easily distinguished by its bright, blood-red colour, on account of which it was named after the Roman God of War. It needs almost two years for Mars to complete one revolution in its elliptical orbit; and we overtake it, usually, once in every 26 months. When Mars, the Sun and the Earth are nearly in a straight line, it is said to be in "opposition"; and this is the most favourable period to study the planet at close quarters. But the distance of Mars from the Earth at opposition varies from 35 million miles (as it is now) to 65 million miles. Naturally, the brightness of the planet varies too, from that of a fourth magnitude star to that of a first magnitude star such as Sirius in the constellation of Canis Major.

Nowadays, Mars outshines all the stars of the sky, including Sirius; but the old man has to bow before the scintillating beauty of Venus, which appears in the west, soon after sunset! The possibility of some kind of "life" existing on these two planets is the subject of serious controversy among the astronomers of the world. But, alas, Venus, the Queen of Beauty, obstinately hides her fair face behind a thick veil of clouds, to the lasting despair of the astronomers! So it is that astronomers in many countries are now eagerly turning their telescopes and cameras to the planet Mars, which gallantly offers itself for a closer scientific study of its mysterious surface.

American Friends of Middle East Hold Student Convention in USA

CHICAGO. — The principal speaker at the first annual convention of Pakistani students attending American universities and colleges was H. E. Syed Amjad Ali, Ambassador of Pakistan to the United States, it was announced by Dr. Edgar J. Fisher, Director of Student Affairs of American Friends of the Middle East which is sponsoring the convention.

The American Friends of the Middle East is an organisation interested in building friendship and understanding between countries like Ethiopia and the United States.

Ato Alemu Begashaw was recently appointed Executive Director of AFME for Ethiopia.

Featured at an evening session was an address by J. Benjamin Schmoker, President of the National Association of Foreign Student Advisers and General Secretary of the Committee on Friendly Relations Among Foreign Students, on the subject: "Sixth Sense in Foreign Student Problems."

According to Dr. Fisher the purpose of the convention is to give an opportunity to Pakistani students to discuss their problems of adjustment which they face upon arrival in the United States and their readjustment to situations in their home country when they return there.

"These Middle Eastern students," Dr. Fisher explained, "come from areas which just now are growing into maturity as autonomous states. This America must realize. They also come from civilizations thousands of years older than our own! This America must also realize.

"The students from the Middle East," he continued, "generally feel that the future of their countries lies within the framework of democracy. They have an avid desire to learn how American democracy works so that they can apply its principles to their own countries."

U.S. Grants Millions For Development in Turkey

WASHINGTON. — A grant of $25 million for farm and manufacturing

---

Swedish Radio Sets Found Cheapest in The World

STOCKHOLM. — Radio sets are cheaper in Sweden than in any other country, the National Federation of Swedish Radio Dealers states in a report based on a large-scale investigation into retail margins.

Arab League to Define Its Attitude Towards Pacts

CAIRO. — The Arab League political committee will meet shortly to define the Arab attitude towards western-sponsored Middle East defense pacts, according to Arab diplomatic circles here. The source said that the Lebanon had summoned the meeting, a date for which would be fixed soon.

Considerable diplomatic activity is now going on in Arab capitals following the visit of Major Salah Salem, Egyptian Minister of National Guidance and Sudan affairs, to King Saud of Saudi Arabia in Riadh and the visit of King Saud this week to King Hussein of Jordan.

President Atassi of Syria sent his Prime Minister, Abdullah El Yaffi, to Amman and President Camillo Shamoun of the Lebanon sent his under Secretary for Foreign Affairs, Fuad Amoun, to Cairo.

The latter's mission, it was stated, was to persuade the authorities of the need to discuss the question of western military assistance to Arab states and the reorientation of Arab policy towards the Pakistan-Turkish alliance.

ETHIOPIAN RED CROSS SOCIETY

RECEIPT AND PAYMENTS ACCOUNTS FOR THE ETHIOPIAN YEAR 1944 AND 1945 (ending 10th September, 1952 and 1953 res-

---

Ethiopian Herald June 19, 1954

THE HIGH-POINT OF US-AFRICAN RELATIONS: BROWN VS. BOARD OF EDUCATION DECISION AND THE VISIT OF HIS IMPERIAL MAJESTY, EMPEROR HAILE SELASSIE I OF ETHIOPIA.

(Below are excerpts from the Jubilee Commemoration Exhibition of His Imperial Majesty Emperor Haile Selassie I First Visit to the United States (1954) presentation at the Marcus Garvey Center in Brooklyn, New York, May 29, 2004)

It has already been stated that His Imperial Majesty's Visit to the United States in 1954 marked the high-point of US-Africa relations. This was represented by the US-Ethiopia Mutual Defense Agreement and the establishment of the Kagnew communications facility which became the major US sigint ("signal intelligence") listening station monitoring all High Frequency radio messages. It was also represented in the linking of the civil rights struggle of Africans in American with the struggle for African Liberation on the African Continent. Sundiata Acoli, an Afrikan Liberation soldier imprisoned in America, writes:

> "Afrikans from Afrika, having fought to save European independence, returned to the Afrikan continent and began fighting for the independence of their own colonized nations. Rather than fight losing Afrikan colonial wars, most European nations opted to grant 'phased' independence to their African colonies. The US now faced the prospect of thousands of Afrikan diplomatic personnel, their staff, and families coming to the UN and wandering into a minefield of incidents, particularly on state visits to the rigidly segregated [Washington] DC capital. That alone could push each newly emerging independent Afrikan nation into the socialist column. To counteract this possibility, the US decided to desegregate. As a result, on May 17, 1954, the US Supreme Court declared school segregation illegal."

Just prior to His Imperial Majesty's arrival in the United States, an editorial in the *Ethiopian Herald* newspaper of May 22, 1954 stated, "So intermeshed are the interests of our present day world that whatever happens in one part may have repercussions in wide areas elsewhere. The United States Supreme Court's decision last Monday on segregated state schools in that country takes its place in this category of events." Sensitive to embarrassment before the world that the spectre of racial segregation, particularly in education, might have during the visit of a Black Emperor of Ethiopia, the US passed the *Brown vs. Board of Education* decision when it did, just one week before His Imperial Majesty's arrival, in order to "show off" the progress the US was making in race relations. According to the United States Government's Amicus Curiae brief to the US Supreme Court,

"It is in the context of the present world struggle between freedom and tyranny that the problem of racial discrimination must be viewed . . . For discrimination against minority groups in the US has an adverse effect upon our relations with other countries. Racial discrimination furnishes grist for the Communist propaganda mills, and it raises doubts even among friendly nations as to the integrity of our devotion to the democratic faith."

The *Chicago Defender* newspaper ran an article during His Imperial Majesty's visit entitled "Integration On Display For Selassie At Capital" and stated that,

"Colored Washingtonians were much in evidence both in official and non official capacities here Wednesday as the nation's capital greeted Emperor Haile Selassie, the Emperor of Ethiopia. . . . The government lost no opportunity to present colored Americans in a favorable light during the Emperor's stay here. It was obvious that the state department realized that his visit on the heels of the Supreme Court decision offered a good opportunity to counter Communist racial propaganda which has plagued this nation in world forums."

A *Cleveland Call and Post* editorial stated that, "The nation's Chief Executive [President Eisenhower] has repeatedly stated that the stigma of racial discrimination is the greatest weakness in our defense against world communism . . . ."

Addressing the issue after receiving an Honorary Doctorate of Laws from Howard University on May 28, Emperor Haile Selassie said, "the World is becoming increasingly aware of the importance of contributions made by colored peoples everywhere to higher and broader standards of social concepts. Events of the recent days, here in the United States, have brilliantly confirmed before the world the contributions which you have made to the principle that all men are brothers and equal in the sight of God."

Asked by a reporter at a New York Press Conference on June 1, 1954 what he thought about the recent United States Supreme Court decision outlawing racial segregation in the public schools, His Imperial Majesty Haile Selassie replied,

"This historic court decision resting on your Constitution will win the esteem of the entire world for the United States. And in particular, it will win the esteem of all the colored people of the world." Asked the same question in San Francisco on June 14, His Imperial Majesty said, "The decision will not only strengthen the ties between Ethiopia and the United States, but will also win friends everywhere in the world."

Another article, which appeared on June 8, 1954, was headlined, "Emperor Selassie Links Negro With Africans Throughout World." According to the *Chicago Defender*, Haile Selassie's Special Message to the African in America:

> "My message to the colored people of the United States is that they continue to press forward with determination their social and intellectual advancement, meeting all obstacles with Christian courage and tolerance, confident in the certainty of the eventual triumph of justice and equality throughout the world. The people of Ethiopia feel the strongest bond of sympathy and understanding with the colored people of the United States. We greatly admire your achievements and your contributions to American life and the tremendous development of this great nation."

Just before the start of Haile Selassie's visit to the US, the British in East Africa launched "Operation Anvil" against the mounting strength of the African Freedom Fighters called "Mau Mau". More than 40,000 British troops captured 26,500 "suspects" and held them in concentration camps. Just over a year later, on December 1, 1955, Rosa Parks embodied that courage and determination and defied Montgomery, Alabama's bus segregation laws by refusing to give her seat to the white man, kicking off the civil rights movement in America. By 1957, Ghana had become the first African nation to achieve its independence.

By January 4, 1965, the New York Times was reporting that Malcolm X had gotten 33 African Heads of State to support his Organization of Afro American Unity (OAAU) petition to the United Nations and that the US State Department, the CIA and the FBI noticed that African leaders were now openly attacking the US

By February 16, 1965, Malcolm X was denouncing the 1954 *Brown vs. Board of Education* decision as "Tokenism":

> "From 1954 to 1964 can easily be looked upon as the era of the emerging African state. And as the African state emerged . . . what effect did it have on the Black American? When he saw the Black man on the [African] continent taking a stand, it made him become filled with the desire to take a stand . . . Just as [the US] had to change their approach with the people on the African continent, they also began to change their approach with our people on this continent. As they used tokenism . . . on the African continent . . . they began to do the same thing with us here in the States . . . . Tokenism . . . every move they made was a token move . . . . They came up with a Supreme Court decision that they haven't put into practice yet. Not even in Rochester, much less in Mississippi."

Relentlessly seeking to educate the African in America about Africa, Malcolm X began making Africa's independence struggle and its relationship to the civil rights struggle a focus of his speeches.

Malcolm X was killed on February 21, 1965. Two weeks later, the New York Times ran a story headlined "World Court Opens Africa Case Monday" which stated that "The International Court of Justice will open oral proceedings Monday in a case linking the segregation struggle of the American Negro and the fate of 430,000 African Bantus and bushmen . . . ." At issue is a four-year effort by Ethiopia and Liberia to bar South Africa from applying her race separation or apartheid doctrine in South West Africa which she controls. The two African complainants, searching for arguments to defeat race-separation policy, have hit on the obvious parallels between the two separations. Almost certainly they will cite the American school segregation cases beginning with the history making decision of May, 1954 in *Brown vs. Board of Education*, in which the Supreme Court found that separate educational facilities are inherently unequal."

Just before Malcolm X's murder, Burundi Prime Minister, Pierre Ngendandumwe, a major supporter of the OAAU petition, was assassinated by Gonzlave Muyinzi, a man who worked at the US Embassy where the CIA was located. Four days after Malcolm X's murder, a Kenyan government official who supported the OAAU petition was assassinated.

Regarding the South West Africa case at the International Court of Justice, at issue was the policy of racial segregation. The San, Khoihoi, Ovambo and Herero tribes lived in general isolation from Europeans until Portuguese explorer Batolomeau Dias landed in 1488. He was followed by hunters, missionaries, explorers and a small number of British and American whalers. The Dutch took over the only deep water port in Namibia (Walvis Bay) but this was taken over by the British in the 18th century. A German merchant called "Ledertitz" set up a town on the coast and it was from this foothold that German South West Africa was established in 1884. In the next three decades, the Germans bought or stole all the land of the natives, and bloodily suppressed African resistance. The biggest uprising against the Germans was made by the Herero, whose revolt in 1904 cost 60,000 lives becoming the first genocide of the Twentieth Century. In 1915, during World War I, the German Colony was conquered by military forces of South Africa. Germany renounced sovereignty over the region in the Treaty of Versailles, and in 1920 the League of Nations granted South Africa a mandate over the territory. The "mandate" stated that the well being and development of those peoples in former enemy colonies not yet able to stand by themselves formed a "sacred trust of civilization" and that "the tutelage of such peoples should be entrusted to advanced nations . . . who are willing to accept it." This meant that the racist white minority of South Africa had, under the Covenant of the League of Nations, accepted the responsibility to do the utmost to promote the material and moral well-being and the social progress of the inhabitants of the country.

In 1946 the United Nations General Assembly requested South Africa to submit a trusteeship agreement to the UN to replace the mandate of the defunct League of Nations; South Africa refused to do so. In 1949, a South African constitutional amendment extended parliamentary representation (and thereby the racist policy of apartheid) to South West Africa. The International Court of Justice, however, ruled in 1950 that the status of the mandate could be changed only with the consent of the UN. South Africa subsequently refused to accede to UN demands concerning a trusteeship arrangement. Aroused by the steps that the government of South Africa was taking to establish apartheid in the mandated territory, Ethiopia and Liberia took the case to the International Court of Justice. It was their contention that, since the Brown vs. Board of Education decision ruled that racial segregation was unfair, did not promote the material and moral well-being and social progress of blacks, and violated their human rights, then applying racial segregation in the form of apartheid in South West Africa could not be said to promote the moral and material well-being and social progress to the black people in that territory, and thus, South West Africa should be granted their independence.

On December 7, 1960, HIM Haile Selassie remarked, in response to a toast by Liberian President William Tubman, that

> "This same spirit of collaboration on problems of mutual concern continuing at an accelerated pace today in the policies which these two African states are pursuing to the end of eradicating racial discrimination, that ignoble and most infamous of prejudices, from the face of the earth. Ethiopia and Liberia are today pressing a legal action before the International Court of Justice at the Hague, for the lifting of the mandate held by the Republic of South Africa over the territory of South-West Africa. We re-affirm here now our determination to pursue this course to its successful conclusion."

On February 2, 1962, HIM Haile Selassie said,

> "The apartheid policy of the racist government of the white minority in South Africa continues to subject our African brothers, who constitute the overwhelming majority in that country, to untold humiliation and oppression . . . .the unfortunate condition in which our African brothers find themselves in South-West Africa under the notorious and deplorable policy of apartheid and ruthless administration of South Africa is equally depressing and intolerable. However, We are convinced that before long the continued efforts of the United Nations and the legal proceedings instituted at the International Court of Justice by our Government and that of our sister state Liberia will bear fruit."

Then, on May 26, 1965, just two months after the murder of Malcolm X and the New York Times article announcing the start of the South West Africa case and linking it with Malcolm X's petition to the United Nations, HIM Haile Selassie said,

> "In South Africa and South West Africa, the policies of apartheid and oppression are becoming increasingly unbearable. The South African Government [Ras note: like the US Government Federal Bureau of Investigations Counter-Intelligence Program or COINTELPRO] is accelerating its ruthless campaign: a methodological campaign of arresting daily, detaining without trial and torturing the Africans and their leaders who are struggling for their fundamental human rights and freedom. All the peace-loving countries of the world must act together to force the colonial governments of South Africa and Portugal to desist from these policies - policies which are inhuman, policies which are detrimental to the peace and security of the ENTIRE WORLD - and grant independence and freedom to these oppressed people."

A year later, while at the Organization of African Unity on July 7, 1966, HIM Haile Selassie said,

> "You are meeting today in this very Hall which gave birth to the Organization of African Unity barely two and a half years ago in order to consider and find a solution to the Southern Rhodesian situation which has posed a grave challenge not only to the OAU but also to the independence of Our individual states and indeed to the national liberation movements of Angola, Mozambique, South West Africa, South Africa, . . . All forces of good, wherever they may be found, must be mobilized to uproot the white supremacists in Rhodesia and in Southern Africa. All freedom loving peoples must co-operate to destroy this deadly cancer of human liberty and equality. After all, at issue is not the loss of freedom to four million Africans but the survival of human liberty. The world, therefore should not condone the perpetration of one of the greatest political crimes in human history."

On July 18, 1966, the International Court of Justice rendered its Judgment in Ethiopia v. South Africa; Liberia v. South Africa:

> "In its Judgment on the second phase of the cases the Court, by the President's casting vote, the votes being equally divided (seven-seven), found that the Applicant States could not be considered to have established any legal right or interest in the subject matter of their claims and accordingly decided to reject them."

Four months later, at the opening session of the OAU on November 6, 1966, His Imperial Majesty Haile Selassie stated:

> "For a number of years now the problem of South West Africa has become the major concern of the African countries. Liberia and Ethiopia, as former members of the League of Nations, acting on behalf of all African States, had sued South Africa for violating her mandate in South-West Africa by introducing the policy of apartheid into that territory and by failing in her obligation to promote the interest of the African population. After six years of litigation, the International Court of Justice decided that the two states did not establish legal status in the case to stand before the Court, thus reversing its judgment of jurisdiction given in 1962. This unfortunate decision has profoundly shaken the high hopes that mankind had placed in the International Court of Justice. The faith man had that justice can be rendered is shattered and the cause of Africa betrayed."

Apartheid laws of South Africa, by this time, had been extended to the country. The UN continued to debate the question, and in June 1971 the International Court of Justice ruled that the South African presence in South West Africa was illegal. However, South Africa continued to govern the territory. As a result, the South West African People's Organization (SWAPO), a black African nationalist movement led by Sam Nujoma, escalated its guerilla campaign to oust South Africans. South Africa continued to resist eviction until December 1988, when it agreed to allow "Namibia" to become independent.

Thus, one can see that the victory of Haile Selassie over Mussolini and the Fascists in 1941, and HIM Haile Selassie's "Coming to America" actually provoked the *Brown vs. Board of Education* decision. The case was significant not only in terms of American history, but in terms of the African Liberation struggle and, therefore, world history. Today, even African American scholars do an injustice by failing to link the Brown v Board of Education decision to the African Liberation struggle led by His Imperial Majesty Emperor Haile Selassie I. As a result, the public is taught that the Brown vs. Board of Education was only a significant element in the civil rights struggle instead of the human rights struggle that Malcolm X was illustrating back in 1964-65.

During this 50th Anniversary of Emperor Haile Selassie I first visit to the United States, the Issembly for Rastafari Iniversal Education (IRIE) has taken up the task of correcting this scholarship and to keep the focus on the brilliant light of the King of Kings and Lord of Lords, His Imperial Majesty Emperor Haile Selassie I.

HIM HAILE SELASSIE'S 1954 REPATRIATION OFFER TO AFRICAN AMERICANS

Jubilee Greetings and Rastafari Blessings from Chicago on June 8, 2004: 1,189 days before the Ethiopian Millennium

Exactly fifty years ago today, Haile Selassie I came to Chicago and made an unscheduled visit to the south side to visit South Park Baptist Church, 3722 S King Drive. I and Sister Myrah decided it was important to go to the church in an attempt to get a "touch"--an insight, an inspiration -- from remembering HIM's presence at that very spot exactly one jubilee later. I&I visit was all the more significant due to the fact that this morning at 6:05 am CST the path of Venus directly crossed over the disc of the Sun, an event known as the Venus Transit. This event happens every 130 years and, according to Kiara Windrider and The Global Oneness Foundation, "The energies of Sun and Venus blend together, and as these blended radiations make their way into the Earth's electromagnetic fields, it weaves the energies of love and unity into the mass consciousness of the planet, and potentially into the hearts of every man, woman, and child alive on Earth!" During this "astronomical event of the year" writes Carl Johan Calleman, PH.D, it is hard to avoid the impressions that the very transit of Venus across the Sun has somehow served to concentrate these energies and has sent an intensifying beam to planet Earth. During the Venus transits the cosmic energies were thus strongly amplified. There are however many good reasons to believe that the Venus transit on June 8, 2004. . . will herald a development of communications between human beings that is not based on technology. The chief reason is that we are now at a stage . . . that favors the right brain half and the intuitive faculties of our mind that are mediated by this. And so, we may expect that the upcoming Venus transit will launch an era of communications utilizing mental rather than electromagnetic fields. . . . Since there is no person alive today who was born in 1882 or earlier the Venus transit in 2004 will be everyone's first such experience. What may we then expect from this occurrence?"

Given that I and Sister Myrah were the only two people able to experience the Venus Transit in the very City where Haile Selassie was a full Jubilee ago, and in the exact location where His Imperial Majesty, the King of Kings and Lord of Lords, Conquering Lion of Judah uttered His special message to the African in American's I raspectfully ask for the attention of the Rastafari Family Worldwide at this time.

Haile Selassie's message spoken at the South Park Baptist Church exactly fifty years ago today was that if the United States has been able to assume its outstanding position as leader in the world today, "it has been due, in no small part, to your [i.e descendants of Africa] profound religious faith and ideals." His Imperial Majesty also said, "The high station which the United States has attained has also been due to the devoted labours of every American citizen. And not the least of the credit for these achievements is due to the numerous groups of American citizens who have made their home on the great African continent of which Ethiopia is proud to be a part." Recalling his 1936 warning to the League of Nations, when Italy was invading his country, Haile Selassie said that in those "difficult hours in our fight for independence, we were not standing alone because peoples of African origin throughout the world were with us in spirit through their moral and spiritual support. It is only natural, therefore, that we Africans should follow with deepest interest the inspiring achievements and contributions of the peoples of African origin in the United States. By your actions, your devotions and your sacrifices you are justifying throughout the world the advancement of the cause of racial and social equality and the right of all peoples to freedom, independence and self-expression."

In His Imperial Majesty's first exclusive interview since His arrival to the United States on May 25, 1954, Emperor Haile selassie told the Chicago Defender newspaper that, "My message to the colored people of the United States is that they continue to press forward with determination, their social and intellectual advancement, meeting all obstacles with Christian courage and tolerance, confident in the certainty of the eventual triumph of justice and equality throughout the world." During the brief but exclusive interview the Emperor also exploded the oft repeated rumor that the people of Ethiopia do not wish to be identified with the colored people of America or associate themselves with their problems. With this rumor in mind, the Emperor, the Emperor was asked, "Is there a kindred feeling between your people and the colored people of America?" The Emperor replied: "The people of Ethiopia feel the strongest bond of sympathy and understanding with the colored people of the United States. We greatly admire your achievements and your contributions to American life and the tremendous development of this great nation. I have been deeply impressed with the warmth of the reception which the colored people of the United States have reserved for me." Next, the Emperor was asked, "What do you feel is the best solution to the unrest found in Africa today?" Emperor Haile Selassie replied, "The orderly progress of the African people toward self-government and the increasing participation by the people themselves in the institutions of their government, is, in my opinion, the best long term solution to the political tensions which exist in parts of Africa where self-determination has not yet been fully achieved. [Ras note: Remember that HIM is speaking in 1954, before even Ghana had independence (1957)-- nine years before the OAU was formed.] The expansion of opportunity for education and the improvement in living standards through development programs will also be important factors in any such program." Finally, the Emperor was asked what had been the highlight of his visit to America thus far. Haile Selassie replied, "I have of course been greatly impressed by the warmth and cordiality of my reception, including of course, the overwhelming warmth of the reception extended me by the colored people of this great nation."

That was His Imperial Majesty Haile Selassie I's message exactly fifty (50) years ago today. This message came at a time when His Imperial Majesty had already invited Africans in America to repatriate to Ethiopia in 1919 (Ethiopian Empress Zauditu's nephew and Commander of the Imperial Army Dedjamatch Nadao's secretary Ato Sinkas to Harlem's Black Jewish leader and Musical Director of the UNIA Rabbi Arnold Josiah Ford); again in 1922 at the UNIA Convention; in 1927 through Dr. Workeneh Martin; and in 1929 to Rabbi Arnold Josiah Ford through Ato Gabrou Desta, who carried Ras Tafari's message that ""We would welcome them back to Ethiopia, their Fatherland . . . . There is plenty of room for them here and we are certain they would be of the greatest aid in restoring their ancient land to its pristine glory."

Recognizing the need of incoming Repatriates to become Citizens of Ethiopia, His Imperial Majesty issued in the Consolidated Laws of Ethiopia that become part of the 1931 Constitution, under Section 9 NATIONALITY 12(2), the following provision providing for Citizenship for Black people of the West:

> "12(2) If the Imperial Ethiopian Government deems any foreigner
> who applies for Ethiopian citizenship to be of value or if it finds
> other special reason which convinces it that the applicant should be
> granted citizenship it may grant him/her Ethiopian citizenship even
> if he/she does not fulfill the [residency and language] requirements
> prescribed in Article 12(b) and (d) of the Nationality Law of 1930."

By 1931, with a framework in place for the full Repatriation of Blacks from the West, Ato Gabrou informed Rabbi Ford and Eudora Paris of land concessions granted. Of course, the Fascist invasion of Ethiopia in 1935-36 interrupted the Repatriation movement of Africans in America until 1948, when, in a letter to the Executive Committee of EWF Local 31 in Kingston, Jamaica, EWF Executive President George Bryan announced the 500 acre Shashemane land grant, which was the personal property of the Emperor, given on a trial basis, "since the way it is utilized will be the touchstone for additional grants." In 1953, His Imperial Majesty sent Madame Sahara on an 18 month repatriation-recruiting mission through Black communities in the United States. A year later, Mamie Richardson of the EWF, went on a similar tour in Jamaica. In the twelve years since His Imperial Majesty regained His Throne in Addis Ababa, Haile Selassie had quadrupled His national economy, Ethiopia was exporting meat, cereals and vegetables to the Middle East, had established a state of the art telecommunications facility in Kagnew, and had made Ethiopian Airlines one of the best and most competitive in the world. That is why Emperor Haile Selassie told a special joint session of the US Congress, on May 28, 1954 that,

> "In consequence, in many respects, and particularly since the last
> world war, Ethiopia has become a new frontier of widely expanding
> opportunities, notwithstanding the tremendous set-back which we
> suffered in the unprovoked invasion of our country nineteen years

ago and the long years of unaided struggle against an infinitely stronger enemy. The last seventeen years have seen the quadrupling of our foreign trade, currency and foreign exchange holdings. Holdings of American dollars have increased ten times over. The Ethiopian dollar has become the only US dollar-based currency in the Middle East today. The assets of our national bank of issue have increased one thousand percent. Blessed with what is perhaps the most fertile soil in Africa, well-watered, and with a wide variety of climates ranging from temperate on the plateau, to the tropical in the valleys, Ethiopia can grow throughout the year crops, normally raised only in widely separated areas of the earth's surface.

Since the war, Ethiopia has become the granary of the Middle East, as well as the only exporter of meat, cereals and vegetables. Whereas at the end of the war, every educational facility had been destroyed, today, schools are springing up throughout the land, the enrollment has quadrupled and, as in the pioneer days in the United States, and indeed, I presume, as in the lives of many of the distinguished members of Congress here present, school-children, in their zeal for education, take all sorts of work in order to earn money to purchase text books and to pursue their education. Finally, through the return in 1952 of its historic ports on the Red Sea and of the long-lost territory of Eritrea, Ethiopia has not only regained access to the sea, but has been one of the few states in the post-war world to have regained lost territory pursuant to post-war treaties and in application of peaceful means and methods. We have thus become a land of expanding opportunities where the American pioneering spirit, ingenuity and technical abilities have been and will contribute to be welcomed."

Agian, on June 8, 1954, His Imperial Majesty told 1,1000 of Chicago's top business, civic and governmenta leaders that, "Unllimited opportunites exist (in Ethiopia) for American capital and pioneering spirit . . . " Having recognised the "no small part" that Africans in America contributed to what Haile Selassie called America's "phenomenal progress", Emperor Haile Selassie I, by the time of His visit to Chicago on June 8, 1954, was well-ready to make good on his "Repatriation Offer" which the Chicago Defender newspaper reported as follows: "a house, rent-free, a salary at least equalling that which applicants are now earning or could earn in America, free transportation to Ethiopia for applicants and their families, annual three-months vacations with pay and -- in some instinces -- automobiles provided by the government. . . . Persons interested in applying for employment in Ethiopia or receiving additional information are advised to write the Ethiopian Embassy in Washington."

Given that June 8, 2004 is a day of intensified energies for mental communications on the Jubilee Anniversary of His Imperial Majesty, the King of Kings and Lord of Lords, Conquering Lion of Judah's presence in the place where I was born and raised, I can't help but to take time to Commemorate the message that the Almighty Himself gave fifty years ago, and its relevance to today. Now, I have a message for the whole Rastafari Family Wordwide.

The message is this:

Exactly fifty years ago, the King of Kings and Lord of Lords came to carry I&I home to a place He Himself had prepared that where He lived, I&I shall abide. It was open to all, yet, even unto today, few have forwarded? Why? Why did I&I fail to claim and manifest I&I deliverance fifty years ago? Ras Mora, during the Jubilee Commemoration Exhibition in Brooklyn, New York, gave the reasoned answer summed up thus: faced with the choice between Repatriation and Integration, the people of African descent in America chose integration. On the heels of the integrated military coming out of World War II and the Korean War, having, apparently, triumphed in the Brown vs. Board of Education decision, We, the Black people of the West, MISSED I&I DELIVERANCE!

Consider this: Ethiopia in 1954 was an emerging world power every bit as much as the United States, who itself had just suffered a "Great Depression" in the late 1920's and early 1930's. Like Ethiopia in 1935-1936, America became embroiled in War in 1941, having been attacked at Pearl Harbor. Today, America is celebrating her "D-Day" victory at Normandy, just as Ethiopians celebrate the Great Ethiopian Anniversary of May 5, 1941 when Emperor Haile Selassie entered Addis Ababa to regain His Throne. Fifty years after the Emperor of Ethiopia came and visited the President of the United States, Ethiopia, the first civilization on earth which gave all peoples religion, science and culture, has now become the last in nearly every major index of quality of life, while America has become the world's only superpower nation.

What happened? Now, fifty years later look at the facts:

Ethiopia is no longer a "well-watered" food exporter with a sky-rocketing economy. Though I&I never give up hope for a glorious Ethiopian future, the fact is that Ethiopia is ravaged by drought, famine, illness, and lack of development. Ethiopia again lost her access to the Red Sea when Eritrea separated. Is this what Haile Selassie envisioned in 1954?

Haile Selassie was recruiting I&I to play no small part in Ethiopia's development, no less than I&I played in America's of which he said I&I had reason to be proud. Thus, I&I have to take some responsibility for the conditions in Ethiopia just as I&I have to take responsibility for conditions in our communities in the west. To the degree that Haile Selassie already set I&I free, so is I&I responsibility at home and abroad. AS the prophet Marcus Mosiah Garvey said in a speech delivered at Madison Square Garden on March 16, 1924:

> "The thoughtful and industrious of our race want to go back to Africa, because we realize it will be our only hope of permanent existence. We cannot all go in a day or in a year, ten or twenty years. It will take time under the rule of modern economics, to entirely or largely depopulate a country of a people, who have been its residents for centuries, but we feel that with proper help for fifty years, the problem can be solved. We do not want all the Negroes in Africa. Some are no good here, and naturally will be no good there . . . . " [Philosophy and Opinions of Marcus Garvey]

What effect has the thoughtful and industrious of the race had on Ethiopia fifty years after Haile Selassie, the King of Kings and Lord of Lords, Conquering Lion of Judah actually came to carry I&I home? From this perspective, one must honestly answer, very little. Did not Haile Selassie have great expectations from I&I? Yes!!! Shashemane has not been developed, additional grants were not given, and "phenomenal progress" in which our ancestors played no small progress has not been achieved.

Thus, the true meaning of the Jubilee Commemoration of His Imperial Majesty Emperor Haile Selassie I First Visit to the United States, 1954, for We, the descendants of Africans in America, is the mercy and forgiveness of His Imperial Majesty for having failed to "Come out of her my people".

As Rasses in America, our God and King came to carry His people home and did not fail to provide everything I&I need for a better life in our Forefather's and Foremother's land. Emperor Haile Selassie came and gave His people citizenship and their "forty acres and a mule" in a Black Empire at a time when America was practicing Jim Crow apartheid. We chose to integrate into America. Our experts, reflecting on fifty year after the Brown v Board of Education decision, have concluded that the situation of public education for Black youth is worse than fifty years ago. Likewise is the situation for Black people in the criminal justice situation, for Black farmers, in every field accept sports and entertainment. In all, the descendants of Africans in America have not become free from the legacy of slavery and racism.

Now, at the outbreak of hostilities against America which started on September 11, 2001 (Ethiopian New Years), the descendants of Africans in America are still second class citizens that have integrated themselves into the judgment which is coming to America. When weapons of mass destruction are used again against America, in America, there will not be any distinction or discrimination made. The integrated African Americans will suffer America's fate right along with her first-class citizens.

I&I are in the same position as descendants of Africans in Europe, who were looking at the outbreak of hostilities in World War II Europe. At that time, enlightened people could see the soon-to-come consequences of failed foreign policies. Haile Selassie himself said at the League of Nations, "Today it is us [Ethiopia], tomorrow it will be you [Europe]. You have struck the match in Ethiopia, but it shall burn Europe!"

Imagine you were a Black person, living in Europe, and foreseeing what was to come. The Voice of Ethiopia, which became the official organ of the Ethiopian World Federation, Inc., as early as 1937, published articles every week foretelling of the "doom" of Europe. All the bombs, air raids, tanks, trenches, dead bodies, millions of dead bodies, war, poverty, famine, millions of dead bodies. Ask anyone to tell of their struggles surviving World War II in Europe . . . . Back then, there was no "Africa for the African's" to Repatriate to. Haile Selassie was himself living in Bath, England! There was no place to run to, to escape to. Haile Selassie had only just begun to prepare a place that where He is, I&I shall abide. Black people in Europe must have been horrified upon the realization that they could not escape the same dark fate that befell Ethiopians at home! Well, that same fate is about to befall America. Yet, descendants of Africans in America were given an opportunity for deliverance in 1954 and instead chose to integrate into America. Not knowing this history, descendants of Africans in America could not properly respond to the destruction of the World Trade Center on September 11, 2001. That is why, in the just published book Paradox of Loyalty: An African American Response to the War on Terrorism edited by Julianne Malveux and Reginna A. Green with a Forward by Cornell West, published by third World Press in Chicago, among the twenty-six (26) submissions purporting to represent the full range of African American Response to the War on Terrorism, none of them express an emigrationist, repatriation response. Given the blighted condition of Black life in America, along with the fact that America was now the target of hostilities and has become the most vulnerable in her history, there is now, more than any period in African American history, reason to embark on a "Back to Africa" program. With diminished quality of life and the impending "doom of America", Repatriation to Ethiopia, our divine heritage as HIM said, represents today, as it did in 1937, our best and last hope for existence itself.

An Open Letter to George W. Bush
May 25, 2004

Mr Bush, as you know, all the inhabitants of the earth live in a new era in which you have ascended to the position of "Commander-in-Chief" of the world's greatest military and to the moral position of "Defender of Freedom and Democracy" for the world. You have declared that you believe that God wants you to be President of the United States in order to assume these roles, and you have also declared your faith in Jesus Christ as your Savior.

The whole world is watching the American Eagle as it claims to be the sole superpower on earth, both militarily and morally, in a new millennium. You, Mr. Bush, are the Chief Eagle. In your nests are advisors and experts from all fields, academic, military, industrial, spiritual and legal Eagles who serve you at this very moment. As the prophet Ezra stated, "On the second night I had a dream, and behold, there came up from the sea an eagle that had twelve feathered wings and three heads. And I looked, and behold, he spread his wings over all the earth. . . . " (2 Esdras 11:1-2a)

Mr Bush, perhaps you would benefit from the advice and counsel of one greater than yourself.

Exactly 50 years ago today, On May 25, 1954, one man made the most extraordinary visit to the United States in her nation's entire history. Never before (and never again) had the United States received such a distinguished visitor. The greatest, most honored man in history, ruler of the world's oldest empire, visited the world's newest superpower nation. Speaking to this most honored guest upon His arrival at the White House, United States President Dwight D. Eisenhower said, "Your Majesty, the American people are honored to have you here on their shores, so that they may salute one who has established a reputation as a defender of freedom and a supporter of progress. For Mrs. Eisenhower and me it is a rare privilege to have you as a guest in this house." At a luncheon later that day, President Eisenhower said, "I think it is safe to say that never has any company here gathered been honored by the presence as their guest of honor of an individual more noted for his fierce defense of freedom and for his courage in defending the independence of his people. . . . I read once that no individual can really be known to have greatness until he has been tested in adversity. By this test, our guest of honor has established new standards in the world."

America's most honored guest was Emperor of the World's Oldest Continuously Sovereign Throne dating from King Ori, 4476 B.C. When the Queen of Sheba bore King Solomon's son Menelik in the 10th century BC, the bloodline as well as the Throne of David was established in His country.

Early in the Fourth Century AD, the Patriarch of Alexandria consecrated Frumentius as the first Bishop in His country. Frumentius then converted King Ezana, making His country one of the earliest Christian nations. The Fall of the Roman Empire at Constantinople to the Ottoman Turks in 1453 AD made His nation the Oldest Christian Nation on earth which survives to this day.

The Emperor had been crowned with the Biblical titles "King of Kings, Lord of Lords, Conquering Lion of Judah" before 72 nations represented by official ambassadors and royal princes (including US Envoy H.M. Jacoby) on November 2, 1930. This made Him the 334th of all the Kings of His country, and the 134th of the Christian Kings of His Empire to sit upon and rule from the actual Throne of David. *TIME* magazine put the Emperor on its June 3, 1930 cover. According to the headline in the June 1931 issue of *National Geographic* magazine devoted to His Imperial Majesty's Coronation, "Haile Selassie the First, Formerly Ras Tafari, Succeeds to the World's Oldest Continuously Sovereign Throne."

On July 20, 1935, the *Chicago Defender* newspaper crystallized the sentiments of the world press when it ran the headline, "Is Ethiopia Stretching Forth Her Hands? Believe the World Headed For Biblical Armageddon." On January 6, 1936, *TIME* magazine named the Emperor its "TIME MAN OF THE YEAR." When Fascist Dictator Benito Mussolini invaded the Emperor's country in early October, 1936, the actual, very real King of Kings and Lord of Lords, the Conquering Lion of Judah was literally at the front of His troops. His country became the first to be liberated against the Axis powers in World War II.

By the time of the of His visit to America in 1954, His Imperial Majesty, the King of Kings, Lord of Lords, Conquering Lion of Judah He had been decorated by the highest military and religious orders of the world. It is therefore significant that New York Mayor Robert Wagner welcomed His Imperial Majesty on June 1st, 1954, saying,

> "My good friends: We pay honour today to a very great man, a man who represents one of the most ancient governments and cultures in the world, and who, with PROGRESSIVE THINKING AND CONSTRUCTIVE PLANNING, has brought his nation to the forefront of modern civilization. The heritage and tradition of 3,000 years of royal lineage encouraged our most distinguished guest of honor to ever greater efforts on behalf of his people and thereby to enormous contributions to the welfare of the world. We honor today an Emperor, a King, the royal leader of a royal country. But His Imperial Majesty, Haile Selassie I, more than Emperor, more than a King, proved himself to be a man, a great man with courage; with vision; with determination; with humanity; and with humility. He gave his ancient nation its first written constitution, relinquishing much of his authority to a Parliament and a judicial system, thereby encouraging the greater development of democracy in his country.

He developed health services, hospitals, schools, a broader education system and lent tremendous encouragement to the recruitment of doctors, nurses, engineers and teachers. His has been a life of understanding and tolerance and his is the mark of true greatness. . . . Your Imperial Majesty, may I say, on behalf of all the people of my city, that we are most happy and most proud to have you with us. You typify that in which we believe. . . . You symbolize the decency and the morality of your country. . . . Welcome, Sir, and God bless you."

On the same day, the King of Kings and Lord of Lords, Conquering Lion of Judah, visited the headquarters of the United Nations becoming the first and the only Head of State to speak both to the League of Nations and the United Nations.

By the time His Imperial Majesty reached Detroit on June 7, He had been awarded the following academic degrees:

1. Honorary Doctor of Philosophy, The National & Kapodistrian University of Athens, Greece, May 4, 1954
2. Doctorate of Polycultural Education, the American University, May 24, 1954
3. Honorary Doctorate of Laws, Howard University, May 28, 1954
4. Honorary Doctor of Laws, Columbia University, June 2, 1954
5. Honorary Doctor of Laws, University of Montreal, June 4, 1954
6. Honorary Doctor of Laws, McGill University, June 5, 1954
7. Honorary Doctor of Civil Laws, University of Michigan, June 7,

While conferring the Doctor of Civil Laws, University of Michigan Vice-President Marvin L. Niehuse said that, "His Imperial Majesty reflects the enviable characteristic of his earlier forbearer -- sagacity and great courage" and called His Imperial Majesty's doctrine of collective security an "enduring monument of history."

A day later, on June 8, Chicago Mayor Martin Kennelly welcomed the Emperor stating, "He is a world figure who symbolizes lion-hearted courage and passionate resistance to aggression and enslavement. In his leadership and example, he stands for the progress of his nation, the prosperity and security of his people and the peace of the world."

By the end of His Imperial Majesty's Visit, the King of King and Lord of Lords, Conquering Lion of Judah had met with America's top military leader Arthur Radford, Head of Joint Chiefs of Staff, U.S. Secretary of State Allen Dulles, Mr. Harold Stassen, head of the Foreign Operations Administration, Major-General Joseph H. Harper and Brigadier-General Carl F. Fritzsche. His Imperial Majesty placed wreaths on the "Tomb of the Unknown Soldier" at Arlington National Cemetery, spoke to a Special Joint Session of Congress, visited Bishop Angus

Dun at the National Cathedral, Reverend Adam Clayton Powell at the Abyssinian Baptist Church, Archbishop Michael at the Hellenic Cathedral of the Holy Trinity Greek Orthodox Church of North and South America, Princeton University and the home of Albert Einstein, lunched with former First Lady Eleanor Roosevelt, inspected industrial and farming sites in the Midwest, the world's largest hydro-electric plant, the Grand Colouee Dam, a Boeing airplane plant, Bremerton Naval Base, the United States Army's Seattle Port, Fort Riley Veteran's Hospital, Yosemite National Park, Long Beach Harbor, 20th Century Fox Film Studios, Fort Benning in Georgia, headquarters of the American Bible Society, the Bronx Zoo, and Yankee Stadium.

Never before or since had one man been accorded so much honor and respect by America's government, business, religious, educational, civic and military institutions. It is no overstatement to say, therefore, that His Imperial Majesty was the greatest human being to set foot in the United States.

Donald Levine, Professor of Sociology at the University of Chicago, states that "there are three reasons why we commonly refer to some happening as a historic event: either it occurs for the first time; it has significant consequences; or it is symbolically important. The importance of His Imperial Majesty's visit does not rest in the mere fact that it was historic for all three reasons just mentioned. When His Imperial Majesty, Emperor Haile Selassie I, came to the United States on May 25, 1954, it was not only historic, it was PROPHETIC.

On June 1, 1954, upon welcoming HIM Haile Selassie I to New York City, United Nations Secretary General Dag Hammarskjold stated, "The Emperor of Ethiopia stands in the perspective of the history of our time as a symbolic landmark, A PROPHETIC FIGURE of the path of man's struggle to achieve international peace and security through concerted international action. I recall the eloquent address Your Majesty delivered before the Assembly of the League of Nations in 1936. Your Majesty then said . . . . . 'It is international morality that is at stake and not the articles of the covenant.'"

New Orleans Mayor deLesseps S. Morrison, on welcoming His Imperial Majesty Haile Selassie I on June 24, stated "If other Chiefs of State had his courage and foresight 20 years ago, many lives would have been saved and the world would not be in its current mess."

Mayor Morrison echoed the sentiments of US Congressman Rep Abraham J. Muller of New York, who stated in the Congressional Record, "The world well remembers that if the free countries of the world HAD COME TO THE AID OF ETHIOPIA when her sovereignty was endangered by the invasion of [Mussolini and the Fascists] the League of Nations might have survived and WORLD WAR TWO MIGHT HAVE BEEN PREVENTED. THAT SHOULD BE A GOOD OBJECT LESSON TODAY."

Thus, here is a "prophetic figure" an actual Davidic Monarch with the Biblical Titles of the Messiah, recognized and honored throughout the world by both high and low, learned and unlearned, even by the post World War II superpowers America and Russia, renowned as a "Prince of Peace", a "Defender of Faith, Freedom and International Morality", uncompromising in Christian principles in the face of the severest adversity and evil ever visited upon man, who prophesied the death of the League of Nations and the collapse of international morality, yet lead the way to the triumph of collective security and the establishment of the United Nations. In all of its significance, His Imperial Majesty Emperor Haile Selassie's 1954 visit to the United States represented the spirit of God made manifest in "King of Kings and Lord of Lords" coming to America, the very real "Second Coming of Christ" which American millenarian preachers, both black and white, had watched, warned and waited for.

If His Imperial Majesty speaks as "A PROPHETIC FIGURE of the path of man's struggle to achieve international peace and security through concerted international action" standing for "the prosperity and security of his people and the peace of the world" as "a world figure who symbolizes lion-hearted courage and passionate resistance to aggression and enslavement" whose life has been one "of understanding and tolerance" and "is the mark of true greatness" having "established new standards in the world" who, "with PROGRESSIVE THINKING AND CONSTRUCTIVE PLANNING, has brought his nation to the forefront of modern civilization" and made "enormous contributions to the welfare of the world" and whom it is said that "If other Chiefs of State had his courage and foresight 20 years ago, many lives would have been saved and the world would not be in its current mess" - if all this is true, then it behooves you, Mr. Bush, to take the time to Commemorate the Jubilee Anniversary of His Imperial Majesty Emperor Haile Selassie I First Visit to the United States in 1954. This is especially true in light of the fact that throughout His visit, His Imperial Majesty taught most prophetically, that the only way to maintain international morality and world peace was through the application of the principles of collective security.

Given that America has and is violating the principles of collective security embodied in international law, is suffering a "high-terror" alert and is the object of increased hatred around the world, it seems as though the leaders in the United States have not learned what US Congressman Rep Abraham J. Muller of New York called "A GOOD OBJECT LESSON TODAY." Since His Imperial Majesty Emperor Haile Selassie is vastly more distinguished, more decorated and by far a more proven and trustworthy steward for the future of the world than any leader today, the American people ought, at this time, to listen and heed the words of His Imperial Majesty Emperor Haile Selassie I. Nothing at this time could be more important to future generations as the prophetic word spoken by the King of Kings and Lord of Lords, Conquering Lion of Judah.

The occasion of the Jubilee Commemoration of His Imperial Majesty Haile Selassie I First Visit to the United States (1954) provides America the perfect opportunity to review the teachings that lead the way to international morality and world peace as taught by the greatest human being that ever graced her shores - His Imperial Majesty Emperor Haile Selassie I. The future, the fate of the world depends upon America's leaders learning and implementing the lesson that His Imperial Majesty taught in 1954 and thereafter.

Mr. Bush, there is much more I would like write to you, but I have limited myself to the scant few facts above. In closing, I would like to remind you that when asked to comment about the Emperor's visit, President Eisenhower replied that it was a very enlightening one and that His Imperial Majesty Emperor Haile Selassie I, the King of Kings and Lord of Lords gave him some very elementary education he should have had before. That you, too, could also receive this enlightenment, I recommend that you read one of the few books which contain the collective speeches of His Imperial Majesty Emperor Haile Selassie I and have the courage to change your foreign policies based on national security to a policy based on "collective security" as taught by and in the spirit of the King of Kings and Lord of Lords, His Imperial Majesty Haile Selassie I. In addition, as the curator of the Jubilee Commemoration Exhibition of His Imperial Majesty's 1954 visit to America, I would be honored to bring the exhibit to the White House.

Mr. Bush, you once said during a presidential campaign debate, that unless someone had experienced salvation in Jesus Christ, that they would not be able to understand what you were saying and what you stand for. Likewise, until one has been enlightened by the King of Kings and Lord of Lords, His Imperial Majesty Haile Selassie I, one can not remain on the true path of international morality and world peace. As "Leader of the Free World", you will be judged according to HIM which in His times He shall show, who is the blessed and only Potentate, the King of kings and Lord of lords . . . .

Most respectfully,
Ras Nathaniel

Printed in the United States
By Bookmasters